BiRD

BRAIN-
TEASERS

Dedicated to the
Fieldston Lower first grade

Quetzal drawing by Jamison

The mission of Storey Publishing is to serve our customers by publishing practical information that encourages personal independence in harmony with the environment.

Edited by Lisa H. Hiley
Book design by Patrick Merrell

Printed in the United States by McNaughton & Gunn, Inc.
10 9 8 7 6 5 4 3 2

Bird
BRAIN-
TEASERS

Patrick Merrell

Storey Publishing

Answers appear directly
after each puzzle spread

ONE OF MY FATHER'S favorite activities during his retirement was watching birds. He was what I like to think of as a bird appreciator, taking delight in just about everything they did.

The main source of his watching was a feeder he'd installed just outside the breakfast room window. It attracted a daily array of scuffers (the term he used for all the smaller birds) as well as blue jays, cardinals, starlings, robins, and one ingenious squirrel who'd found a way past all his anti-squirrel measures. Mourning doves and the rest of the local squirrel population would mop up the leftovers below.

Such was his love of all things avian that my sister-in-law made him the quilt shown on the next page as a birthday gift one year.

That appreciation of birds is reflected in the text that follows as well as the wide variety of crosswords, brainteasers, word puzzles, sudoku, acrostics, quizzes, and visual puzzles. Enjoy!

—*Patrick Merrell*

WHAT IS IT
about a little bundle
of feathers, with beak on
one end and sticks for legs
on the other, that makes
us at once peaceful and
calm and pleased with
the world?

BIRDS are
one of the most
successful animals
the world has ever seen. They
have survived for over 100 million
years, singularly mastering without aid the land, sea, and air. They
live in almost every environment
the planet has to offer, from harsh
Antarctic expanses to barren
deserts, from bustling cities to
remote and unforgiving seas.

But perhaps even
more impressive is
the unparalleled beauty
of their songs and appearance.
These traits have served as
inspiration throughout history,
woven into the literature, songs,
symbols, and legends of ethnic
and political groups as varied as
the species themselves. In short,
birds are both works of art and
marvels of engineering.

TWEET CROSSING

Insert one bird from the list into each box so that two words are spelled, one reading across and one down. Three birds will not be used. Cover the bird list for an extra challenge.

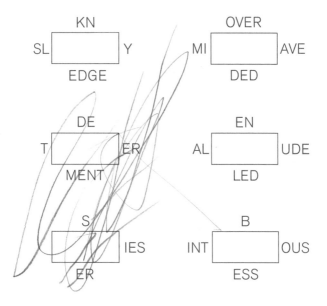

KN
SL [   ] Y
EDGE

OVER
MI [   ] AVE
DED

DE
T [   ] ER
MENT

EN
AL [   ] UDE
LED

S
[   ] IES
ER

B
INT [   ] OUS
ESS

COOT	EAGLE	LOON	ROBIN
CROW	EGRET	OWL	TERN
DIVER	EMU	RAIL	TIT
DOVE	IBIS	RAVEN	WREN

BAL

SA [ ] KEEPER

ING

B

L [ ] R

SEMENT

P

DIS [ ] G

AF

FRA [ ] ITY

OON

BIO

[ ] SION

SITY

H

AL [ ] CUS

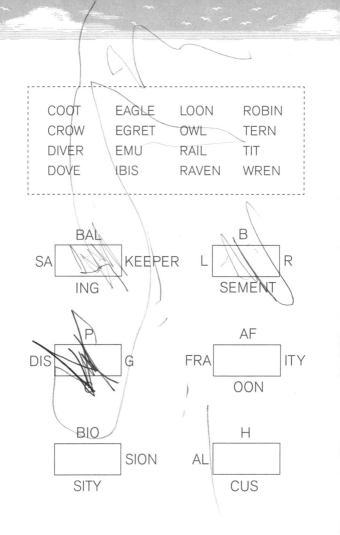

TWEET CROSSING

OWL	KNOWLEDGE, SLOWLY
RAIL	DERAILMENT, TRAILER
COOT	SCOOTER, COOTIES
CROW	OVERCROWDED, MICROWAVE
TIT	ENTITLED, ALTITUDE
RAVEN	BRAVENESS, INTRAVENOUS
LOON	BALLOONING, SALOONKEEPER
ROBIN	PROBING, DISROBING
DIVER	BIODIVERSITY, DIVERSION
EMU	BEMUSEMENT, LEMUR
TERN	AFTERNOON, FRATERNITY
IBIS	HIBISCUS, ALIBIS

IAN FLEMING'S spy, agent 007, was named after the noted American ornithologist James Bond (1900–1989).

Fleming, an avid birdwatcher living in Jamaica, was looking for an ordinary name and chose Bond's from the cover of one of his favorite bird books, *Birds of the West Indies*.

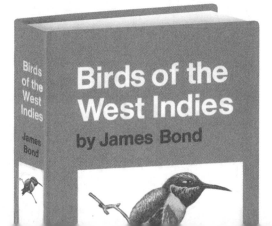

*One of my favorite images
of our small, beautiful world
is of morning's first light
sweeping around the globe,
continuously, relentlessly,
forever circling and returning
to repeat the cycle. Always,
somewhere, it is dawn, and
always, somewhere,
the birds are singing.*

DON KROODSMA
Birdsong expert and author of *The Singing Life of Birds*

ARCHAEOPTERYX, dating back 150 million years, is the oldest known bird. Although possessing reptilian features such as toothed jaws, a tail with vertebrae, and clawed fingers on its wings, it had feathers, a feature unique to birds.

The first "true birds" came about 50 million years later. They included ichthyornis, a small flier resembling a tern, and hesperornis, a flightless, loonlike diver the size of a small seal.

A German farmer discovered this archaeopteryx fossil in the 1870s and sold it soon after in exchange for a cow. Known as the *Berlin specimen*, it's now on display in the Naturkunde-museum in Berlin.

FOR THE BIRDS

ACROSS

1 "Washboard" muscles
4 The ___ Nineties (era)
7 Health resort
10 "i" topper
11 Scooby-____
12 Paintings
13 Promenade where loud birds congregate?
15 "Fo fum" preceder
16 Not lenient
17 Politician Barack
19 Psychic's gift
21 Mine finds
22 Listening device worn in the henhouse?
26 Sty cry
27 At this very moment
28 Chip dip with zip
30 Increase
34 Meteor suffix
35 Where a black bird might wet its whistle?
37 Cracker or hatch starter
38 Small amount
39 Actress Longoria
40 Double curve
41 James Bond, for one
42 "You betcha"

DOWN

1 Descriptive wds.
2 Gull's resting spot at sea, sometimes
3 Eyelid ailment
4 Birthplace of Poland's Solidarity
5 "You've got mail" co.
6 Singer Ono
7 Expedition where one might see oxpeckers
8 First coat of paint
9 "Relax, soldier!"
14 Submerged vessels, but not by design
18 Hound sound
20 Cob's mate
22 Trig function
23 Temporary suspension, as for a TV show
24 Coastal coves
25 Bad answer to "Who's there?"
29 Parts of *The Seagull*
31 Follow orders
32 Goalie's feat
33 Ensnare
36 Knock, as in "The Raven"

BONUS SCRAMBLER

Unscramble the letters in the light green squares to answer this clue: Joint that attracts white birds.

＿ ＿ ＿ ＿   ＿ ＿ ＿ ＿

FOR THE BIRDS

Bonus Scrambler: SWAN DIVE

In Trees

with apologies to Joyce Kilmer

I think that I have never heard
A singer lovely as a bird.

A bird, who clad in colored vest,
Nestles in its treeborne nest;

A bird that beckoned by the skies,
Lifts its feathered arms and flies;

A bird that calls out in rejoice,
To bathe the heavens with its voice.

There's little doubt that God conferred
His sweetest songs upon the bird,

But must these minstrels e'er display them
Saturday morning at five AM?!

Dodo Drawings

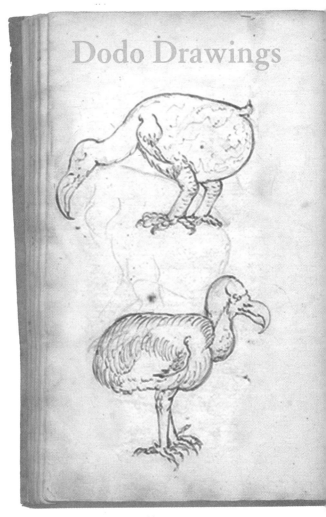

Depicted here are three drawings of a dodo from a journal on *De Gelderland,* a Dutch East Indies Company ship that visited the dodos' island home of Mauritius (500 miles east of Madagascar) around 1601.

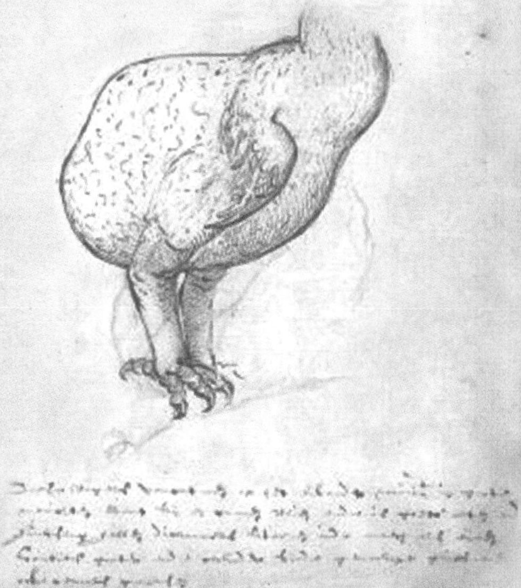

Bird Is the Word

TURKEY: Because Guinea fowl were once imported through Turkish territory, Europeans commonly called them turkeys. The term made its way across the Atlantic when similar birds were found in the New World.

LARK: In the Middle Ages, when young men and maids laid out nets in the morning to catch larks, they sometimes got distracted, and *larking* soon became a term for frolicking about.

JAYWALKING has nothing to do with birds. The term comes from "jay" meaning a rube, likely one unused to big city streets.

STOOL PIGEON appears to be a term that came from the practice of tying actual pigeons to stools to lure others of its kind.

COCKPITS in airplanes were named for their cramped resemblance to the pits used for cockfights.

DUCK, meaning to lower one's head, comes from the Old English *ducan,* "to dive." The bird was given the name later.

SCRAMBLED EGGS

Unscramble the names of the songbirds that laid these eggs. Transfer the circled letters, in order, to the boxes at the end to answer this: What do you call birds that make nests in chimneys?

DIE BLURB

_ _ _ _ _ _ _ _

BROIL MEAT
ROE OIL

_ _ _ _ _ _ _ _ _

_ _ _ _ _ _

FLINCH DOG

_ _ _ _ _ _ _ _ _

KINGDOM CRIB

_ _ _ _ _ _ _ _ _ _

HACKED ICE

_ _ _ _ _ _ _ _ _

OWL SLAW

_ _ _ _ _ _ _ _

CLAN RAID

_ _ _ _ _ _ _ _ _

LOW LYE
BRAWLER

_ _ _ _ _ _ _

_ _ _ _ _ _ _

ALARMED WOK

_ _ _ _ _ _ _ _ _ _ _

DIRT CAB

_ _ _ _ _ _ _

ART CELS
GNAT EAR

_ _ _ _ _ _ _

_ _ _ _ _ _ _

SCRAMBLED EGGS

BLUE**B**IRD
BALTIMO**RE** ORIOLE
GOLDF**I**NCH
MO**C**KINGBIRD
CHIC**K**ADEE
SWAL**L**OW
CARDIN**A**L
YELLOW WARBLER
M**E**ADOWLARK
CATBI**RD**
SCARLET TANAGER

BRICK LAYERS

THE BEATLES' SONG, "Blackbird," features about ten seconds of a real blackbird singing. The bird's song was reportedly from a sound effects record titled *Volume Seven: Birds of a Feather.*

*Each bird
loves to hear
himself sing.*

ARAPAHO PROVERB

The bird who
has eaten cannot
fly with the bird
that is hungry.

OMAHA PROVERB

DURING WORLD WAR II, the U.S. used a pigeon corps of 54,000 birds for carrying messages. More than 3,000 soldiers, known as pigeoneers, trained and cared for them.

The birds were parachuted from airplanes, released from subs, flew day or night, and sometimes carried cameras to take reconnaissance photographs.

BIRD WATCHING

Study the drawings below. Flip the book over and, without looking back, see if you can identify two *substituted* drawings on the next page.

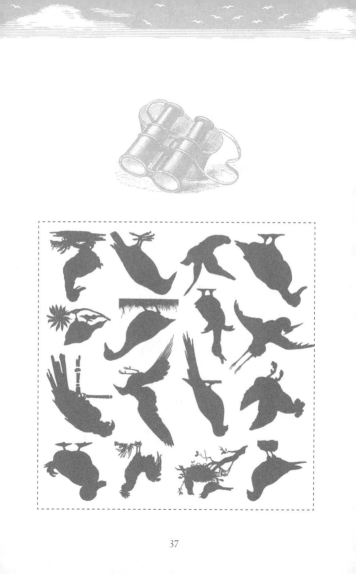

BIRD WATCHING

**ALTHOUGH
NEARLY TASTELESS,**
worms provide birds
with a good supply
of juicy protein.

water: 80%   protein: 14%

nitrogen, oil, and ash (each): 2%

You acid-blue metallic bird,
You thick bird with a strong crest
Who are you?
Whose boss are you, with all your
   bully way?
You copper-sulphate blue-bird!

D.H. LAWRENCE
excerpt from "The Blue Jay"
Birds, Beasts and Flowers: Poems (1923)

Pretty in Pink

Fresh out of art school, Don Featherstone was hired by Union Products in 1957 to create a new line of lawn ornaments. Working from *National Geographic* photos, one of Don's first creations was the now famous pink plastic flamingo (*phoenicopteris ruber plasticus*).

Although the birds were an instant hit, it took a 1984 appearance on TV's *Miami Vice* to boost flamingo sales past those of Don's very first creation, a white duck. All told, 20 million of the flamingos, which come in two poses, have been sold since their introduction.

To honor Don for his contribution to the lawns of America, the company added his signature to the design in 1986. The place of honor? The flamingo's rear end.

HHs

Like "hen house," each of these answers has the initials HH. Use the clues to fill in each answer, then read down the circled letters to find the answer to this: Where do hens work?

1. Music style
2. Big boss, informally
3. Captain's rope-pulling command
4. Neighborly bit of aid
5. Lofty aspirations
6. After-work bar special
7. Wham-O fad of the '50s
8. Pack animal's complaint
9. Stay-at-home dad
10. A United States president
11. Top secret

1. H __ __   H __ __

2. H __ __ __   H __ __ __ __ __

3. H __ __ __ __   H __

4. H __ __ __ __ __ __ __   H __ __ __

5. H __ __ __   H __ __ __ __

6. H __ __ __ __   H __ __ __

7. H __ __ __   H __ __ __

8. H __ __ - H __ __ __

9. H __ __ __ __   H __ __ __ __ __ __

10. H __ __ __ __ __ __   H __ __ __ __ __

11. H __ __ __ - H __ __ __ __

45

HHs

1. H**I**P HOP
2. HEAD HO**N**CHO
3. H**E**AVE HO
4. HELPIN**G** HAND
5. HI**G**H HOPES
6. HAP**P**Y HOUR
7. HU**L**A HOOP
8. HEE-H**A**W
9. HOUSE HUSBA**N**D
10. HERBER**T** HOOVER
11. HU**S**H-HUSH

IN EGGPLANTS

TO GIVE A HOOT is
thought to have evolved
from the phrase "I don't
care a hooter for him"
(hooter meaning an
iota or whit).

MARK TWAIN
(1835–1910)

*Noise proves nothing. Often
a hen who has merely laid
an egg cackles as if she has
laid an asteroid.*

*It is better to be a
young June-bug
than an old bird
of paradise.*

....

*She was not quite what you
would call refined.*

*She was not quite what you
would call unrefined.*

*She was the kind of person
that keeps a parrot.*

Birds **Watch** Birds

These lines might give one a sense of
déjà vu. That's because the sentences are
the same when read in reverse order.

MOURNING doves
and whistling SWANS
heard CRANES whooping
and gulls LAUGHING.
The BURROWING owls
SPOTTED
some
SPOTTED
owls BURROWING. The
LAUGHING gulls and
whooping CRANES heard
SWANS whistling and
doves MOURNING.

BIRDOKU 1

These nine letters fill
the grid nine times each:

LADY ROBIN

Each letter must appear once in each row,
in each column, and in each 3×3 square.

The letters highlighted in green, reading down,
will spell out the answer to this riddle:

What has a beak, two wings, and
sees equally well from both ends?

A _ _ _ _   _ _ _ _

	D	A		N	R			
R		Y				N	B	
	O		A	B	L			R
	B				O			Y
		R	L		Y	B		
O			R				A	
D			O	L	A		Y	
	I	L				O		B
			B	R		A	L	

BIRDOKU 1

B	D	A	Y	N	R	L	O	I
R	L	Y	I	O	D	N	B	A
N	O	I	A	B	L	Y	D	R
L	B	D	N	A	O	R	I	Y
I	A	R	L	D	Y	B	N	O
O	Y	N	R	I	B	D	A	L
D	R	B	O	L	A	I	Y	N
A	I	L	D	Y	N	O	R	B
Y	N	O	B	R	I	A	L	D

A BLIND BIRD

The language of birds is very ancient, and, like other ancient modes of speech, very elliptical: little is said, but much is meant and understood.

GILBERT WHITE
English naturalist (1720–93)

A SERINETTE, or bird organ, was a hand-cranked musical device used by French ladies of the 17th and 18th centuries to teach songs to their pet canaries. A bellows blew air into a set of pipes, regulated by a rotating barrel lined with pins.

LADY BIRD JOHNSON, whose real first name was Claudia, got her lifelong nickname as an infant when her nurse declared that she was as "purty as a ladybird." The reference wasn't actually to a bird but to the brightly colored beetle more commonly called a ladybug.

Lady Bird at about age 3 (circa 1915)

God gave a loaf
to every bird,
but just a crumb
to me.

EMILY DICKINSON (1830–86)
"God Gave a Loaf to Every Bird"

HEAD SCRATCHERS 1

----

1. See if you can unscramble AOPRTR to spell two different six-letter birds:

   — — — — — —

   — — — — — —

2. One day, an egg fell from a robin's nest. A hard sidewalk was directly below, and yet the egg fell ten feet without breaking. It wasn't caught or cushioned in any way. How was this possible?

3. A common black Eurasian bird is missing from this pangram, a sentence that uses every letter of the alphabet at least once. See if you can figure out what it should be.

__ __ __ __ __ __ __S LOVE

MY BIG SPHINX OF QUARTZ.

4. Can you think of a bird that contains the name of its young and its female within its letters? The two words read from left to right, although one is not in consecutive order.

HEAD SCRATCHERS 1

1. RAPTOR and PARROT
2. The nest was more than ten feet above the sidewalk, therefore the egg hadn't broken yet.
3. JACKDAWS
4. CHICKEN contains CHICK and HEN.

IN THIS 1890 GAME, players waddle around a gameboard in the hopes of being the first to arrive back at the nest, where a Golden Egg awaits.

TV Quotes

[Lucy gets caught spying on the neighbors]

Lucy Ricardo:

I was, uh . . . birdwatching!

Ricky Ricardo:

Birdwatching?

Lucy Ricardo:

Uh, yeah! Do you know that there's a yellow-bellied woodpecker on our lawn?

Ricky Ricardo:

No, but I know that there's a red-headed cuckoo in the living room.

LUCILLE BALL and **DESI ARNAZ**
I Love Lucy (1951)

I tawt I taw a puddy tat! Isn't it about time you saw something else? Sth-tupid bird....

SYLVESTER to TWEETY

Marge:

Homer, there's a bird on your head.

Homer:

I know, Marge, he's grooming me.

THE SIMPSONS (1989)

Please, now that all pretenses are off, call me Penguin — a flightless bird, but one with style.

THE PENGUIN in *The Batman* (2004)

From the Sears, Roebuck Catalogue

These are a few of the bird-hunting supplies offered by the "cheapest supply house on earth" in its 1902 catalogue.

BIRD CALLS.

No. 6R4560 Allen's Latest Improved Wood Duck Caller, the most natural toned, easiest blowing. **Used in the field by the best duck shooters in America.** Each...........35c

No. 6R4563 Duck Calls, B. G. I. with rosewood mouthpiece, horn tip. Good quality. Price. each...............22c

No. 6R4565 Turkey Calls, horn tip with rosewood mouthpiece, calls by sucking into it. Each...........................25c

If by mail, postage extra, each, 3 cents.

Snipe Call.

No. 6R4567 Snipe Calls, made of best horn and a perfect snipe call. Each....18c

If by mail. postage extra, each, 2 cents.

No. 6R4570 Fuller's Metallic Wild Goose Caller. Very good, Each...........75c
If by mail, postage extra, 5 cents.

Collapsible Ducks.

No. 6R4600 Collapsible Canvas Decoy. A good imitation of the natural duck. Made of best canvas, beautifully painted in natural colors, waterproofed, inflated with air, and when not in use the air can be let out and ducks folded. Weight, 4 ounces, each. Packed one dozen in a neat wooden box, 2¾x9 inches. **We sell in any quantity.** Mallards, red heads, canvas backs and blue bills. Per dozen. **$5.45**

Grass Suits. Reduced to 90 cents.

90c PER SUIT is our price, and thousands are now being worn by sportsmen everywhere.

No. 6R5112 For wild goose, duck and all kinds of shore bird shooting; made of long tough imported marsh grass into cape coat with hood. They weigh less than four pounds, are convenient to wear and shoot from. Make good waterproofs in rainy weather, are easily packed and carried. Hunters appreciate the value of these suits, as no blind or bough house is necessary when shooting on marshes. Weight, about 5 pounds.

Single suits, each...................................90c

BIRDS ON A WIRE

Arriving at work one Monday morning, a man noticed two birds sitting on a wire across the street. When he left that evening, there were four. On the following four days he noticed there were always double the number of birds on the wire in the evening compared to the number in the morning.

If the total number of birds he saw for all five days was 48 (adding together all the morning and evening tallies), and the number of birds in the morning was never the same, what were the five morning tallies?

BIRDS ON A WIRE

The morning tallies were two on the first day
and then (in whatever order) one, three, four,
and six birds for the other mornings.

$$(2+4) + (1+2) + (3+6) + (4+8) + (6+12) = 48$$

THE WOODCOCK, whose eyes are set high and far back, has a nearly 360-degree range of vision without moving its head.

OWLS have fixed eyes that often afford them no more than a 110-degree view, but their heads can rotate up to 270 degrees.

I'd rather you shot at tin cans in the back yard, but I know you'll go after birds. Shoot all the bluejays you want, if you can hit 'em, but remember it's a sin to kill a mockingbird. . . . Mockingbirds don't do one thing but make music for us to enjoy. They don't eat up people's gardens, don't nest in corncribs, they don't do one thing but sing their hearts out for us.

HARPER LEE
Atticus Finch in *To Kill a Mockingbird* (1960)

Sing Like a Bird

F. Schuyler Mathews deemed the hermit thrush's song "the grand climax of all bird music" when he put a bit of the bird's repertoire into musical notation in 1910.

"Rendered on a piano these phrases convey only a very faint suggestion of the matchless beauty of the song. A very fine flute or a piccolo, if perfectly handled, or a violin with skillful use of harmonics, would more nearly suggest the singer's tone."

DOWN TIME

ACROSS

1 H.S. grads-to-be
4 Tree a Mississippi kite might nest in
7 *Audubon*, e.g., for short
10 Try to win over
11 A Stooge
12 Univ. Web address tag
13 Predictably
15 Born as
16 Penny filling, these days
17 Sugar measures (abbr.)
18 Warm, dry spots for bird watching softies
22 Chirp
23 Fall activity for many North American birds
29 Like migrating penguins
30 College sports org.
31 Cote note
32 Spring and fall, e.g.
35 Env. enclosure
36 Real estate professional (abbr.)
37 The Big Apple's biggest newspaper (abbr.)
38 Lion suffix
39 *The Wizard of Oz* studio
40 Negative vote

DOWN

1 Southeast African people after whom a country was named
2 Violin bow application
3 Noise
4 Down Under bird
5 Mauna ___
6 Actor Gibson
7 High I.Q. group
8 Masterful
9 "Wild" estimate
14 Nova ___
17 Rockies range
19 Possess
20 Bylaw, for short
21 His, to ornithologist François Le Vaillant
23 Aesop's *The Crow and the Raven*, e.g.
24 Exams for future D.A.'s
25 Dozens of months
26 The Huskies of the Big East, for short
27 Singer Tucker
28 Overly quick
32 *The Muppet Show* eagle
33 Chick's first home
34 Bill dispenser

Crossword grid (15 columns wide):

1	2	3	■	4	5	6	■	7	8	9
10			■	11			■	12		
13		14					■	15		
16				■		17				
18			19	20	21					
■		22						■		
23	24	25					26	27	28	
29			■			30				
31			■	32	33	34				
35			■	36			■	37		
38			■	39			■	40		

BONUS ANSWER

The letters in the light green squares, reading left to right, will spell out a flock sometimes seen 23-Across.

_ _ _ _   _ _ _ _ _

DOWN TIME

S	R	S		E	L	M		M	A	G
W	O	O		M	O	E		E	D	U
A	S	U	S	U	A	L		N	E	E
Z	I	N	C				T	S	P	S
I	N	D	O	O	R	S	E	A	T	S
		T	W	E	E	T				
F	L	Y	I	N	G	S	O	U	T	H
A	S	E	A			N	C	A	A	
B	A	A		S	E	A	S	O	N	S
L	T	R		A	G	T		N	Y	T
E	S	S		M	G	M		N	A	Y

Bonus Answer: SNOW GEESE

78

TWO DECOYS, a preening pintail drake and a sleeping Canada goose, created in the early 1900s by master carver A. Elmer Crowell, sold for a record-setting $1.1 million *each* in 2007.

The Brum* and the Oologist

This abridged 1891 poem from Britain's *Punch*, a satirical magazine,
takes a swipe at oologists (egg collectors).

The "Brum" and the Oologist
Were walking hand in hand;
They grinned to see so many birds
On cliff, and rock, and sand.
"If we could only get their eggs,"
Said they, "it would be grand."

"Oh, Sea-birds," said the Midland man,
"Let's take a pleasant walk!
Perhaps among you we may find
The Great — or lesser — Auk;
And you might possibly enjoy
A scientific talk."

The skuas and the cormorants,
And all the puffin clan,
The stormy petrels, gulls, and terns,
They hopped, and skipped, and ran
With very injudicious speed
To join that oily man.

"The time has come," remarked the Brum,
"For 'talking without tears'
Of birds unhappily extinct,
Yet known in former years;
And how much cash an egg will fetch
In Naturalistic spheres."

"But not our eggs!" replied the birds,
Feeling a little hot.
"You surely would not rob our nests
After this pleasant trot?"
The Midland man said nothing but, —
"I guess he's cleared the lot!"

"Well!" said that bland Oologist,
"We've had a lot of fun.
Next year, perhaps, these Shetland birds
We'll visit — with a gun;
When — as we've taken all their eggs —
There'll probably be none!"

*Brum is slang for a resident of Birmingham, England

Oology was a popular hobby around the turn of the century
in both Europe and the United States.

Fall Migration

83

HEAD TO TAIL

Twenty-two birds are hiding in the grid, but there's a twist: The last letter of one bird's name is the first letter of the next. It's a continuous chain, so the 22nd bird you find will connect back to the first. Words read forward, backward, up, down, and diagonally. Cover up the word list for an extra challenge.

AUK	LAPWING
DOVE	NIGHTHAWK
EAGLE	NIGHTINGALE
EGRET	RHEA
EIDER	ROBIN
EMU	RUFF
FIRECREST	TEAL
GODWIT	TERN
HARRIER	THRUSH
KINGFISHER	TIT
KITE	UMBRELLA BIRD

```
G  R  E  T  S  E  R  C  E  R  I  F
D  O  E  U  E  H  S  O  B  I  E  F
O  K  D  K  N  A  K  P  U  L  M  U
G  N  I  W  P  A  L  A  A  L  U  R
O  O  R  O  T  E  R  G  E  M  M  E
D  T  D  E  R  O  N  T  I  G  B  D
W  I  R  K  O  I  I  T  R  M  R  I
I  N  V  A  T  K  I  T  K  G  E  E
T  E  I  H  U  U  U  A  U  U  L  G
G  I  G  G  H  A  E  H  R  G  L  R
I  I  T  S  H  R  T  E  A  R  A  U
N  I  H  O  R  T  I  E  A  G  B  A
I  O  R  K  S  R  H  G  V  E  I  H
B  R  U  E  R  O  U  A  K  O  R  R
O  O  S  A  F  I  K  T  W  O  D  O
R  E  H  S  I  F  G  N  I  K  O  N
```

HEAD TO TAIL

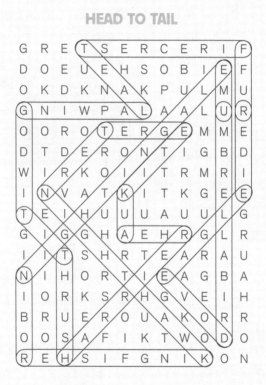

SONGBIRDS learn their vocalizations rather than being born knowing them. A fledgling listens to his elders, continually refining the arrangement of notes until it matches.

Egg Sizes

It would take over 2,000 hummingbird eggs, the world's smallest, to equal the weight of just one ostrich egg.

HUMMINGBIRD
½" long / .02 oz.

OSTRICH
6" long / 3 lbs.

CHICKEN
2¼" long / 3 oz.

Although the ostrich egg is the world's largest, it's the smallest in comparison to the size of its mother.

Big as the ostrich's egg is, it's still less than half the length of eggs that were laid by the elephant bird, a 10-foot tall behemoth that became extinct around the 16th century.

About the year of Our Lord 1420 an Asian junk . . . on a crossing of the Sea of India towards the Isle of Men and Women . . . saw the egg of a bird called roc, the egg being as big as a seven gallon cask, and the size of the bird is such that from the point of one wing to another was sixty paces and it can quite easily lift an elephant or any other large animal.

FRA MAURO, Venetian monk (1460)
Translated excerpt from the enlarged section
of his world map on the next page (south is up).
Some believe the roc to be the now extinct elephant bird.

FOWL DEFINITIONS

Each bird below can fit one of the clues on the next page. Match them up by writing the numbers in the blank spaces. Go ahead, don't be chicken.

A ___ Albatross
B ___ Bunting
C ___ Cardinal
D ___ Chat
E ___ Coot
F ___ Crane
G ___ Crow
H ___ Darter
I ___ Dipper
J ___ Duck
K ___ Eagle
L ___ Goose
M ___ Grouse

N ___ Hawk
O ___ Kite
P ___ Nutcracker
Q ___ Parrot
R ___ Pigeon
S ___ Quail
T ___ Rail
U ___ Rook
V ___ Skimmer
W ___ Snipe
X ___ Swallow
Y ___ Swift
Z ___ Turkey

1 Speedy
2 Complain
3 Imitate
4 Wearisome burden
5 Shrink back in fear
6 Talk
7 Ladle-like utensil
8 Two on a par 4
9 Patriotic drapery
10 Peddle wares
11 Child's toy
12 Straw hat
13 Believe, naively

14 Swindle
15 Paramount
16 Brag
17 Quick mover
18 Geezer
19 One easily duped
20 Dodge, as duties
21 Silly one
22 Hoisting machine
23 Shell-breaking tool
24 Failure
25 Criticize sneakily
26 Rant or scold

FOWL DEFINITIONS

A	4	Albatross	**N**	10	Hawk
B	9	Bunting	**O**	11	Kite
C	15	Cardinal	**P**	23	Nutcracker
D	6	Chat	**Q**	3	Parrot
E	18	Coot	**R**	19	Pigeon
F	22	Crane	**S**	5	Quail
G	16	Crow	**T**	26	Rail
H	17	Darter	**U**	14	Rook
I	7	Dipper	**V**	12	Skimmer
J	20	Duck	**W**	25	Snipe
K	8	Eagle	**X**	13	Swallow
L	21	Goose	**Y**	1	Swift
M	2	Grouse	**Z**	24	Turkey

THE CANARY ISLANDS were named for a large breed of dog found there. *Insularia Canaria,* the Latin name, means "Island of Dogs." The native yellow birds were named later, after the island, after the dogs.

The Canary Islands' coat of arms

PENGUINS are unmatched in the bird world for their diving capabilities. Although abundant food can generally be found during short, shallow dives of three minutes or so, the emperor penguin holds the record for staying below: 18 minutes.

THE OPENING SCENE OF *E.T.*, set in California, features the haunting call of an eastern screech owl — a bird as lost as E.T. was since it would have been hundreds, if not thousands, of miles from its home turf.

The early bird gets the worm — but what about the early worm?

ALFRED E. NEUMAN
Mad's Half-Wit and Wisdom

GREEN EGGS, NO HAM

Start at the blue egg in the upper left and move either straight across or straight down, stopping at any green egg. Move perpendicularly from that green egg to another green egg. Continuing in this fashion, find a path to the blue egg in the lower right.

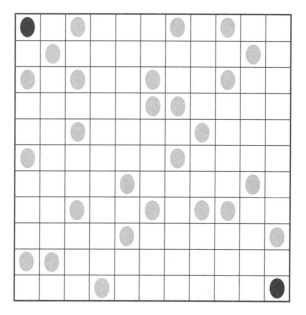

GREEN EGGS, NO HAM

Here's the shortest route:

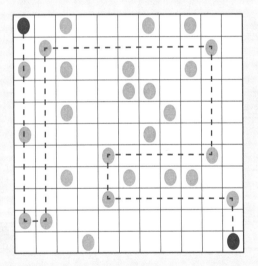

Fall is my favorite season in Los Angeles, watching the birds change color and fall from the trees.

DAVID LETTERMAN
(born 1947)

THE BIRDS OF AMERICA, Audubon's four-volume 26½" × 40" masterpiece, was financed almost entirely by Audubon himself. Over a period of 14 years he raised $115,640 — equivalent to more than $2 million in today's dollars.

THE BIRDS OF AMERICA;

from

ORIGINAL DRAWINGS

By

JOHN JAMES AUDUBON,

Fellow of the Royal Societies of London & Edinburgh and of the
Linnæan & Zoological Societies of London
Member of the Natural History Society of Paris of the Lyceum of New York,
&c. &c. &c.

Published by the Author.

Walgvogel:

That's Dutch for dodo. It translates to "nasty bird," which is what 16th century Dutch sailors called the bad-tasting fowl. Although dodos were easily captured and eaten, the main reasons for the bird's demise were more likely the destruction of its forest habitat and the introduction of pigs, cats, dogs, rats, and macaques that plundered the dodo nests.

Dodos (actual size here)
stood about three feet tall.

FEATHERED FRIENDS

The words below are spelled using the letters in BIRD WATCHERS. There's only one way to fit them all in the grid.

2 letters

AD
AS
AT

3 letters

AIR   RED   SIT
ARC   SAC   THE
DEW   SEA
ICE   SET

4 letters

ACRE   RATE
BEAT   WEST
DRAW   WIRE
HERB

5 letters

BEACH
BIRCH
CREST
STRAW
WATER
WHEAT

6 letters

BATHES
BREAST
HABITS
RACERS
WADERS

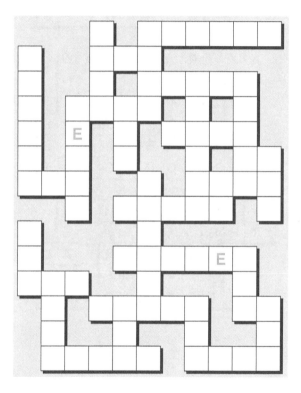

FEATHERED FRIENDS

A few anagrams of BIRD WATCHERS:
CATBIRD SHREW
BIRCH STEWARD
WE CHART BIRDS

COAL MINE CANARIES appear to have been rarely used in the United States, where the Davy's Safety Lamp (shown) and, later, the methanometer were preferred. In England, however, the birds were employed in mine pits as recently as the 1980s. British mine

workers often grew quite attached to their singing coworkers, and should one of their voices fall silent, an airtight door on its box would quickly be shut and the bird revived with oxygen.

Be Casso-wary

The five-foot tall Australian cassowary is considered the world's most dangerous bird. When threatened or harrassed, it will aggressively attack with its long dagger-like claws. Because of the bird's ability to maim and even kill, zookeepers regard it as one of the most dangerous of *any* type of animal to keep.

Unfortunately, humans are an even bigger threat to cassowaries than vice versa. The significant inroads that have been made into the bird's natural forest habitat increasingly expose it to traffic accidents, disease, stress, and dog attacks.

One ray of hope is a reserve in Mission Beach, Queensland, that provides a haven for cassowaries and many other birds, butterflies, mammals, and rare plants.

A Mission Beach road sign

God gives every bird his worm, but He does not throw it into the nest.

P. D. JAMES
English mystery novelist (born 1920)

OLIVIER MESSIAEN wrote "Exotic Birds" in 1956, a musical composition that combines the birdcalls of 38 North American birds as well as those from China, India, Malaysia, and the Amazon. Two years later he completed his "Catalog of Birds," a series of 13 movements featuring the voices of 77 distinct birds.

FLOCKS

Many terms have been coined for flocks, flights, dissimulations, voleries, or groups of birds. Count yourself above average if you can match up more than half of these.

1 Ostentation of	_____	**A**	Chickens
2 Gaggle of	_____	**B**	Nightingales
3 Parliament of	_____	**C**	Goldfinches
4 Brood of	_____	**D**	Owls
5 Murder of	_____	**E**	Starlings
6 Charm of	_____	**F**	Larks
7 Exaltation of	_____	**G**	Geese
8 Conspiracy of	_____	**H**	Peacocks
9 Watch of	_____	**I**	Ravens
10 Murmuration of	_____	**J**	Crows

FLEDGLINGS

Most names for young birds are pretty easy to figure out, such as owlet, eaglet, or peachick. These six are less obvious.

1 Young swan   ____   **A** Cast
2 Young falcon   ____   **B** Eyas
3 Young hawk   ____   **C** Cygnet
4 Young rooster   ____   **D** Squab
5 Young partridge   ____   **E** Cheeper
6 Young pigeon   ____   **F** Cockerel

FLOCKS

1 H Ostentation of peacocks
2 G Gaggle of geese
3 D Parliament of owls
4 A Brood of chickens
5 J Murder of crows
6 C Charm of goldfinches
7 F Exaltation of larks
8 I Conspiracy of ravens
9 B Watch of nightingales
10 E Murmuration of starlings

Alternate names also used:
muster of peacocks; skein or wedge of geese;
wisdom of owls; clutch or peep of chickens;
ascension or chattering of larks;
unkindness of ravens.

FLEDGLINGS

1 C Swan, cygnet
2 A Falcon, cast
3 B Hawk, eyas
4 F Rooster, cockerel
5 E Partridge, cheeper
6 D Pigeon, squab

THE
SYNCHRONIZED
swooping and turning
of bird flocks en masse
is really not that much
different from
sports spectators
performing
"the wave"
in a stadium.
The individual
birds see and
sense a change
in movement
and respond
accordingly.

There
are
two
ways
to
shoot
a bird.

One
leaves
the bird
free to
laugh
at the
shooter
another
day.

Back page advertisement from
The Bird Book by Chester A. Reed (1915):

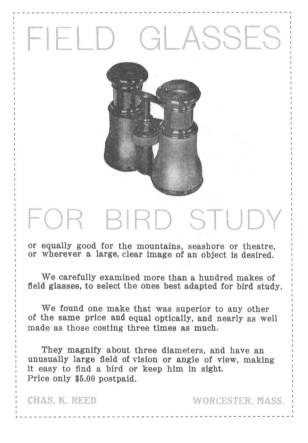

*I'm
frightened of eggs,
worse than frightened,
they revolt me. That white
round thing without any
holes . . . have you ever seen
anything more revolting than an
egg yolk breaking and spilling
its yellow liquid? Blood is
jolly, red. But egg yolk is
yellow, revolting.*

ALFRED HITCHCOCK
(1899–1980)

CHAIN LETTERS

Enter a single word on each line that's connected in some way to the word above and below it. For example, TOP could follow LAP (laptop) and precede HAT (top hat). Clues define the single word on each line. Each page is a separate puzzle. The one on the next page has two parts to it.

BIRD

Nourishment   _____

Battle   _____

Not opposed to   _____

At any time   _____

Traffic light color   _____

Small vegetable   _____

Rooster   _____

Cow's fly swatter   _____

FEATHER

Book material   _____

Jet   _____

Cop's handout   _____

Paned item   _____

Mall activity   _____

Picnic carrier   _____

Rug maker   _____

Phone   _____

Support   _____

Japan or Jamaica   _____

Golfer's need   _____

Bubbly drink   _____

Pool filler   _____

Primary   _____

LAND

CHAIN LETTERS

BIRD	FLY
FOOD	PAPER
FIGHT	(AIR)PLANE
FOR	TICKET
EVER	WINDOW
GREEN	SHOPPING
PEA	BASKET
COCK	WEAVER
TAIL	BIRD
FEATHER	CALL
	BACK
	COUNTRY
	CLUB
	SODA
	WATER
	MAIN
	LAND

FOUR EARLY VERSIONS of
the Great Seal of the United
States featured a rooster, a
dove, a two-headed eagle, and
a phoenix in flames. Congress
finally approved this sketch,
made by Charles Thomson,
on June 26, 1782.

If men had wings and bore black feathers, few of them would be clever enough to be crows.

REV. HENRY WARD BEECHER
(1813–87)

Peeping Hot

Sing a song of sixpence,
A pocket full of rye;
Four and twenty blackbirds,
Baked in a pie.

Odd as it may sound, the inspiration for this verse might be a 16th-century fad of hiding surprises in dinner pies. One Italian cookbook of the time actually included a recipe "to make pies so that the birds may be alive in them and flie out when it is cut up." The result would be to create "a diverting Hurley-Burley amongst the Guests."

China's Pests

The *Great Sparrow Campaign* was a plan instituted in 1958 by Mao Zedong. The goal was to rid China of its tree sparrows, the flying "pests" which each year ate tons of grain intended for China's growing and hungry populace.

The only problem was that the tree sparrows ate more insects than they did grain and the locust population exploded, causing widespread famine. Mao's decree was rescinded two years later, but not soon enough to prevent the killing of 9 million birds and the deaths of 38 million people from starvation.

FLYING
INSTRUCTIONS

Answer the clues on the next page,
then transfer the letters to the same-
numbered spaces in the grid. A bit of
sage advice from English naturalist,
William Henry Hudson, will be revealed.

1B	2D	3E		4G	5F	6A	7C	8D	9A	
10E	11A	12D		13D	14A	15B	16G		17E	18D
19F	20E	21A	22B	23G		24F	25A	26C	27D	
	28D	29A	30B		31B	32D	33E	34D	35A	
36D	37G		38C		39A	40D	41B	42G		

A. Imitating a bird

$\overline{39}$ $\overline{29}$ $\overline{14}$ $\overline{35}$ $\overline{9}$ $\overline{11}$ $\overline{25}$ $\overline{6}$ $\overline{21}$

B. Every seven days

$\overline{31}$ $\overline{30}$ $\overline{41}$ $\overline{15}$ $\overline{22}$ $\overline{1}$

C. Picnic crasher

$\overline{38}$ $\overline{7}$ $\overline{26}$

D. The study of birds

$\overline{2}$ $\overline{40}$ $\overline{18}$ $\overline{32}$ $\overline{28}$ $\overline{27}$ $\overline{36}$ $\overline{13}$ $\overline{8}$ $\overline{34}$ $\overline{12}$

E. Flora and . . .

$\overline{10}$ $\overline{20}$ $\overline{3}$ $\overline{33}$ $\overline{17}$

F. Amaze

$\overline{5}$ $\overline{24}$ $\overline{19}$

G. Yard enclosure

$\overline{37}$ $\overline{23}$ $\overline{42}$ $\overline{4}$ $\overline{16}$

FLYING
INSTRUCTIONS

A. WHISTLING

B. WEEKLY

C. ANT

D. ORNITHOLOGY

E. FAUNA

F. AWE

G. FENCE

YOU CANNOT
FLY LIKE AN
EAGLE WITH
THE WINGS
OF A WREN

William Henry Hudson (1841–1922) was born in Buenos Aires and emigrated to England in 1870. His best known work is *Green Mansions*, a romance novel set in the jungles of Venezuela.

Bird migration is the one truly unifying natural phenomenon in the world, stitching the continents together in a way that even the great weather systems, which roar out from the poles but fizzle at the equator, fail to do.

SCOTT WEIDENSAUL
Living on the Wind (1999)

White House Pets

Many U.S. presidents have had
pets of the avian persuasion.

Washington: Polly the parrot

Jefferson: Dick the mockingbird sang
German and French folk songs, perched
on the president's shoulder, and hopped
up the stairs after him.

Madison: Polly the macaw was fed by a
window for daily onlookers to watch.

Taylor: Johnny Ty the canary

Buchanan: two bald eagles

Lincoln: Jack the
turkey was saved
from the Thanks-
giving table by
pleas from one of
Lincoln's sons.

Grant: roosters
and a parrot

Delivery of a Harding turkey

Hayes: four canaries and a mockingbird
Cleveland: canaries and mockingbirds
McKinley: a Mexican double-yellow-headed parrot
Teddy Roosevelt: Eli Yale the blue macaw, Baron Spreckle the hen, a barn owl, two parrots, and a one-legged rooster
Wilson: chickens
Harding: canaries and a turkey
Coolidge: Nip and Tuck the canaries, Snowflake the white canary, Old Bill the thrush, Enoch the goose, and a mockingbird
Kennedy: Robin the canary, Bluebell and Marybelle the parakeets
Lyndon Johnson: lovebirds

Roosevelt's rooster

AN OSTRICH'S
eyeball is the size
of a tennis ball.

It's not a record setter, though. In 2007,
scientists measured a collosal squid's eye at
four times as large, or the size of a soccer ball.

Somewhere over
the rainbow
Bluebirds fly.
Birds fly over the
rainbow.
Why then, oh why
can't I?

"OVER THE RAINBOW"
The Wizard of Oz
(recorded October 7, 1938)

ONE AT A TIME

Change one letter at a time to connect each set of words. For example, getting from BEAK to PECK using one word could be done this way: BEAK - PEAK - PECK

CHEEP to TWEET
using 3 words

CHEEP

_____

_____

_____

TWEET

WING to FEET
using 4 words

WING

_____

_____

_____

_____

FEET

BIRD to CATS
using 3 words

BIRD

_____

_____

_____

CATS

TREE to FLEW
using 2 words

TREE

_____

_____

FLEW

NEST to WORM
using 4 or 5 words

NEST

_____

_____

_____

_____

_____

WORM

WREN to TERN
using 3 words

WREN

_____

_____

_____

TERN

EGG to FLY
using 10 words

EGG

_____

_____

_____

_____

_____

_____

_____

_____

_____

_____

FLY

DUCK to SWAN
using 7 words

DUCK

_____

_____

_____

_____

_____

_____

_____

SWAN

ONE AT A TIME

Although there are a few variations, we've given only one solution for each. Congratulations if you can find others.

CHEEP	TREE	DUCK	EGG
SHEEP	FREE	PUCK	EGO
SHEET	FLEE	PUNK	AGO
SWEET	FLEW	PUNT	ADO
TWEET	•	PENT	ADD
•	NEST	SENT	AID
BIRD	WEST	SEAT	BID
BARD	WENT	SWAT	BAD
BARS	WANT	SWAN	SAD
BATS	WART	•	SAY
CATS	WARM	WREN	SLY
•	WORM	WHEN	FLY
WING	IN 4:	THEN	
WIND	NEST	TEEN	
FIND	WEST	TERN	
FEND	WENT		
FEED	WONT		
FEET	WORT	(WERT, an archaic form	
	WORM	of "be," can also reduce	
		this solution to 3.)	

ON MARCH 13, 2000, a reputed member of the Genovese crime family, Anthony "Tough Tony" Federici, was arrested for twice firing a 20-gauge shotgun from the roof of his Queens, New York, restaurant.

A mob hit?

No. Mr. Federici was trying to protect his champion racing pigeons, kept on the restaurant's roof, from a pair of circling hawks. He was released after paying a $90 fine for hunting within the city limits.

Cheep Money

Many of the world's
currencies have birds
depicted on them.
Here are just a few.

Left page from top: Bahamas, Gambia, Guatemala, Qatar; this page from top: Macedonia, Indonesia, Antarctica (not legal tender)

J.M. BARRIE
(1860–1937)

The reason birds can fly and we can't is simply that they have perfect faith, for to have faith is to have wings.

"Do you know,"
Peter asked, "why
swallows build in
the eaves of houses?
It is to listen to
the stories."

- - - - - - - - - -

PETER PAN

I'm youth, I'm joy,
I'm a little bird that has
broken out of the egg.

BEFORE BIRDS

Answers to asterisked (*) clues
are words that can precede "bird."

ACROSS

1 Vast amount*
4 *Silent Spring* pesticide
7 Loud squawker*
10 Mil. base stores
11 Brazilian port, for short
12 Form suffix
13 Kind of sale in late December
15 1,150 in old Rome
16 Disgorged
17 Luau paste
18 Sweetheart*
20 Starter for log or center
22 Arizona to Maine dir.
23 Bad luck symbol*
27 More than none
28 One who bares all
31 Moral failing
32 Resolve, as differences
34 Italian suffix
35 Cone bearer
36 Harper Valley org.
37 Milk source*
38 Loooong time
39 Day brightener*

DOWN

1 Black or white *Mad* bomber
2 Split personalities?
3 Pronto
4 ___ blank (was stumped)
5 Supped
6 Hot rum drink
7 Get aboard the bandwagon
8 Recess
9 New Haven student
14 Historical find
19 Admit
20 Pacific event that causes odd weather
21 Online buyer's button
23 Fundamental
24 Whittler's tool
25 Unusual collectible
26 Decorate
29 Absorbs, with "up"
30 Skirt that covers only the hips
33 Beachgoer's souvenir

BONUS SCRAMBLER

Unscramble the letters in the light green squares to find a slang term for liquor. The term can be divided into two words, each of which can precede "bird."

_ _ _ _ _ _ _ _ _

BEFORE BIRDS

Both words in 18- and 23-Across can precede "bird."

S	E	A		D	D	T		J	A	Y
P	X	S		R	I	O		U	L	A
Y	E	A	R	E	N	D		M	C	L
	S	P	E	W	E	D		P	O	I
		L	A	D	Y	L	O	V	E	
	E	P	I			E	N	E		
B	L	A	C	K	C	A	T			
A	N	Y		N	U	D	I	S	T	
S	I	N		I	R	O	N	O	U	T
I	N	O		F	I	R		P	T	A
C	O	W		E	O	N		S	U	N

Bonus Scrambler: FIREWATER
(firebird, water bird)

Come, fill the Cup, and
in the fire of Spring
Your Winter garment
of Repentance fling:
The Bird of Time has
but a little way
To fly — and Lo! the
Bird is on the Wing.

- - - - - - - - - - - - -

OMAR KHAYYAM
The Rubaiyat (circa 1122)
translated by Edward FitzGerald (1868)

Emu Trivia

Impress your friends with these emu facts:

Emus can run 30 mph and jump straight up 7 feet.

Emus are good swimmers.

Neither the emu nor the kangaroo, its mate on Australia's coat of arms, can walk backwards.

Emus have small claws at the end of each wing.

An emu's body contains three gallons of oil.

Mozart's Bird

In 1784, a month after Wolfgang Amadeus Mozart had completed his piano concerto no. 17 in G Major, K. 453, he was startled to hear a section of it being whistled in a local shop — by a starling!

Mozart visited the shop often and was known to whistle in public, perhaps explaining the incident. Whatever the reason, he bought the bird and kept it as a cherished pet. Three years later when it died, a full funeral was held and Mozart recited the poem at left that he wrote specially for the occasion:

Here lies a foolish darling,
A bird called Starling.
Amid life's full glow
He came to know
Death's stinging pain.
My heart, I feel it drain
To think him dead.
Oh reader! Please shed
A tear, it's sad.
He was never bad;
Always spirited and gay,
At times, I'd even say
A mischievous sport,
But not a loutish sort.
He's already above,
To sing his praise of love
For the friendship that we
Both gave for free.
It was so unexpected,
By death to be collected,
Thinking not in farewell
Of he who rhymes so well.

AVIAN SHORTHAND

See if you can identify the birds represented here. For example, **turkE** would be turkey.

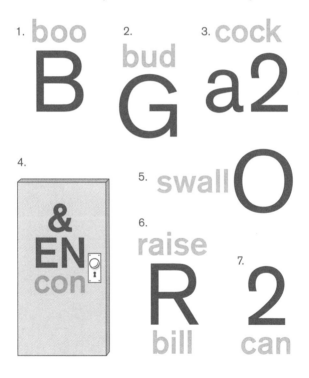

1. boo B

2. bud G

3. cock a2

4. & EN con

5. swall O

6. raise R bill

7. 2 can

8. can  E

9. C deeter

10. phen

11. it

12. rob

13. e moo

14. nye 10 gail

AVIAN SHORTHAND

1. Booby
2. Budgie (name commonly used for a budgerigar, a popular pet parakeet)
3. Cockatoo
4. Andean condor
5. Swallow
6. Razorbill
7. Toucan
8. Canary
9. Seedeater
10. Peahen
11. Parrot
12. Robin redbreast
13. Emu
14. Nightingale

IT'S A MIRACLE OF NATURE that one can hold in the palm of the hand a sprightly sprig of a creature whose ancestors were flitting over the heads of dinosaurs more than 100 million years ago.

Hey, what's this bird, this falcon that everybody's all steamed up about?

HUMPHREY BOGART
The Maltese Falcon (1941)

BIG BIRD AND DONALD DUCK are the only fictional characters to have both stars on the Hollywood Walk of Fame and signatures in the cement forecourt of Grauman's Chinese Theater.

NASA and Birds

Because of the Kennedy Space Center's close proximity to the Merritt Island National Wildlife Refuge in Florida, NASA has undertaken a number of steps to deal with birds during liftoff. Special avian radar tracks larger birds, nearby roadkill is removed so as not to attract vultures, grass is cut near the launch site, and a trap-and-release plan has even been employed on launch day. The stakes are high, since a collision could endanger the space shuttle and the crew inside it... not to mention the life of one very unfortunate bird.

Birds flock around the space shuttle during rollout.

HEAD SCRATCHERS 2

- -

1. Add only Os to spell five bird names:

WDCCK _____

CNDR _____

SNW GSE _____

WD STRK _____

SNWY WL _____

2. Can you rearrange these letters to spell a bird's name?

AABDEIMNRS _____

3. One day, two fathers and two sons went bird watching in the woods. Each saw a different red-headed woodpecker, and yet a total of only three red-headed woodpeckers were seen by them. How could this be?

4. See if you can fill each blank with the same word:

   _____ got a _____ for having

   the bird's _____ mended.

5. Can the average owl see things farther away at night or during the day?

HEAD SCRATCHERS 2

1. WOODCOCK
   CONDOR
   SNOW GOOSE
   WOOD STORK
   SNOWY OWL
2. A BIRD'S NAME
3. It was a threesome: a son, father,
   and grandfather.
4. BILL
5. At night. The sun is the most distant
   thing an owl can see during the day.
   At night, it can see stars that are much
   farther away.

BIRDS CAN SEE a world of color far richer than we can. Humans have only three types of cones in each eye, whereas birds have four. Since each type interprets visual input differently, the picture formed in a bird's brain contains colors, including some in the ultraviolet range, that we can only imagine.

Not Much Afoot

A number of birds have
little or no ability to walk.

• Hummingbirds use their feet only to
perch or scratch themselves. Moving even
a few feet is done by flying.

• Swifts' legs are almost nonexistent and
their tiny clawed feet are suited for little
more than clinging to vertical surfaces.

• The legs of some water birds, such as
grebes and loons, are set so far back for
diving and swimming that walking or
even taking off from land isn't possible.

• Frigate birds do almost everything aloft,
including sleep, and have tiny feet that are
nearly useless for walking. About the only
time they come to earth is to breed.

The word stupid *is utterly inapplicable to any bird with which I am acquainted . . . It is only when birds of any species are unacquainted with man, that they manifest that kind of ignorance or innocence which he calls stupidity.*

JOHN JAMES AUDUBON
(1785–1851)

Look at this word:

FIJI

Now you can say
you've seen a blue jay
with green eyes in Fiji.

TWELVE DAYS

According to the lyrics of "The Twelve Days of Christmas," a partridge was sent on the first day — and then again on each of the next 11 days. By song's end, a dozen partridges would be cluttering up someone's doorstep, or parlor, or wherever one would keep all these chirping gifts.

Given that two turtledoves arrived on each of the second through twelfth days, and many of the other days saw French hens, calling birds, geese, and swans also being delivered, how many birds did "my true love" end up sending?

On the twelfth day of Christmas,
My true love sent to me
Twelve drummers drumming,
Eleven pipers piping,
Ten lords a-leaping,
Nine ladies dancing,
Eight maids a-milking,
Seven swans a-swimming,
Six geese a-laying,
Five golden rings,
Four calling birds,
Three French hens,
Two turtledoves,
And a partridge in a pear tree!

TWELVE DAYS

There'd be a total of 184 birds.
The individual totals would be:

12 partridges (1×12)
22 turtledoves (2×11)
30 French hens (3×10)
36 calling birds (4×9)
42 geese a-laying (6×7)
42 swans a-swimming (7×6)

Birds are so much more maneuverable than our airplanes are today. Birds can hover, they can fly backwards and sideways. And insects— oh forget it!—upside down, loop-de-loop, all sorts of things.

ANNA MCGOWAN

program manager for the Morphing Project
at NASA's Langley Research Center

BIRDS are a popular animal when it comes to flag design. Eagles, two-headed and otherwise, account for the great bulk of avian symbols, but everything from the albatross to the white-tailed tropicbird fly on flagpoles around the world.

Guatemala's quetzal

Uganda's crane

Ecuador's condor

Albania's two-headed eagle

Midway Islands' albatross

I wish the Bald Eagle had not been chosen the Representative of our Country. He is a Bird of bad moral Character . . . The Turkey is in Comparison a much more respectable Bird, and withal a true original Native of America . . . He is besides, though a little vain & silly, a Bird of Courage, and would not hesitate to attack a Grenadier of the British Guards who should presume to invade his Farm Yard with a red Coat on.

BENJAMIN FRANKLIN
writing to his daughter, Sally (January 26, 1784)

A turkey is more occult and awful than all the angels and archangels . . . If you go and stare at a live turkey for an hour or two, you will find by the end of it that the enigma has rather increased than diminished.

GILBERT K. CHESTERTON (1874–1936)
English author and champion for Catholicism

LIKE SOME . . .

ACROSS

1 Floor washer
4 Letter afterthoughts
7 Tend to the lawn
10 "Ungodly" belief
12 Knuckle-walker in the jungle
13 Like some lamps
15 Hoped-for store sale turnouts
16 Savannah predators
17 "The Greatest" in the ring
18 Irish native
20 Like some sentries
24 Veered from the facts
25 Make a dress
27 Monthly release of *Bird Talk*
30 ___ fool (go nuts)
31 Like some beauties
34 Prez married to Mamie
35 Hybrid with fragrant flowers
36 One of 100 in D.C.
37 Noise-squelching sound
38 Oz. and mg.

DOWN

1 Molten rock
2 Peter of *Lawrence of Arabia*
3 Fear of birds, e.g.
4 Bakery buy
5 Nine-digit I.D.
6 Used one's nose
7 Speedy shark
8 Sesame preceder, in a phrase
9 Unites
11 Egret's neck shape
14 Word before slicker
18 Ones billed by lawyers
19 Wide shoe width
21 It can put two and two together
22 Money held by a third party
23 Really hate
26 Fishes, à la herons
27 Colored eye part
28 Fermented rice drink
29 Classic Nordic men's name
30 Tire filler
32 Cynical laugh sound
33 Word said for a doctor

BONUS SCRAMBLER

Unscramble the letters in the light green
squares to answer this clue: Like some who run

_ _ _ _ _ _ _ - _ _ _ _ _ _

LIKE SOME . . .

M	O	P		P	S	S		M	O	W
A	T	H	E	I	S	M		A	P	E
G	O	O	S	E	N	E	C	K	E	D
M	O	B	S			L	I	O	N	S
A	L	I		C	E	L	T			
	E	A	G	L	E	E	Y	E	D	
		L	I	E	D		S	E	W	
I	S	S	U	E		A	C	T	A	
R	A	V	E	N	H	A	I	R	E	D
I	K	E		T	E	A	R	O	S	E
S	E	N		S	H	H		W	T	S

Bonus Scrambler: CHICKEN-LIVERED

182

Happier of happy
though I be, like
birds I cannot take
possession of the
sky, mount with a
thoughtless impulse,
and wheel there, one
of a mighty multitude
whose way and motion
is a harmony and
dance magnificent.

WILLIAM WORDSWORTH
(1770–1850)
The Recluse

All the World's a Bathtub

During a Pacific storm on January 10, 1992, a shipment of 29,000 Chinese-made plastic ducks, turtles, beavers, and frogs spilled overboard. Some 19,000 of the Friendly Floatees bath toys, as they were known, headed for the sunny beaches of South America, Australia, and Indonesia. The remaining 10,000 floated north and hit Alaska that fall.

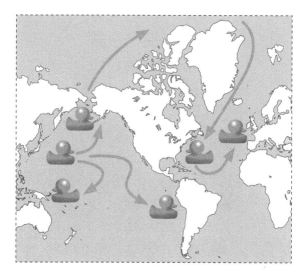

Ten years later, after finding their way through the Bering Strait and across frozen Arctic waters, a few intrepid ducks made it past Greenland and washed up on the eastern U.S. coast. Several unconfirmed sightings were also reported on the shores of Britain, but no one there has yet collected on the $100 bounty offered by the manufacturer for a recovered toy.

Country birds
in lush trees perch.
City birds
for trees must search.

Country birds
fat worms eat up.
City birds
on old crusts sup.

Country birds
in blue skies flit.
City birds
tall buildings hit.

Country birds
with others tweet.
City birds
with horns compete.

Country birds
the good life scored.
But city birds
are never bored.

PLUS A TO Z

Unscramble the letters in each
equation to spell a bird's name.

A + GLEE = __ __ __ __ __

B + IRON = __ __ __ __ __

C + EARN = __ __ __ __ __

D + CROON = __ __ __ __ __ __

E + HAT SNAP = __ __ __ __ __ __ __ __

F + CHIN = __ __ __ __ __ __

G + TREE = __ __ __ __ __ __

H + HURTS = __ __ __ __ __ __

I + RED BULB = __ __ __ __ __ __ __ __

J + BUY ALE = __ __ __ __ __   __ __ __

K + SORT = __ __ __ __ __

L + OVERBID = _ _ _ _ _ _ _ _

M + TRAIN = _ _ _ _ _ _

N + FOCAL = _ _ _ _ _ _

O + OILER = _ _ _ _ _ _

P + ARROWS = _ _ _ _ _ _ _

Q + A BUS = _ _ _ _ _ (one bird's young)

R + HONE = _ _ _ _ _

S + ATLAS ORB = _ _ _ _ _ _ _ _ _

T + CHOIRS = _ _ _ _ _ _ _

U + OGRES = _ _ _ _ _ _

V + NEAR = _ _ _ _ _

W + BARREL = _ _ _ _ _ _ _

X + IN HOPE = _ _ _ _ _ _ _ (myth)

Y + ROPES = _ _ _ _ _ _

Z + ILL ARBOR = _ _ _ _ _ _ _ _ _

189

PLUS A TO Z

A	EAGLE	N	FALCON
B	ROBIN	O	ORIOLE
C	CRANE	P	SPARROW
D	CONDOR	Q	SQUAB
E	PHEASANT	R	HERON
F	FINCH	S	ALBATROSS
G	EGRET	T	OSTRICH
H	THRUSH	U	GROUSE
I	BLUEBIRD	V	RAVEN
J	BLUE JAY	W	WARBLER
K	STORK	X	PHOENIX
L	LOVEBIRD	Y	OSPREY
M	MARTIN	Z	RAZORBILL

Autumn Birds

The wild duck startles like a sudden thought
And heron slow as if it might be caught
The flopping crows on weary wing go bye
And grey beard jackdaws noising as they flye
The crowds of starnels wiz and hurry bye
And darken like a cloud the evening sky
The larks like thunder rise and suthy round
Then drop and nestle in the stubble ground
The wild swan hurrys high and noises loud
With white necks peering to the evening cloud
The weary rooks to distant woods are gone
With length of tail the magpie winnows on
To neighbouring tree and leaves the distant crow
While small birds nestle in the hedge below

JOHN CLARE
(1793–1864)

CHRISTMAS BIRD COUNT *n.* A year-end migration of wooly-capped binocular users

into wooded areas of the Western Hemisphere. One theory suggests it's a century-old ritual involving the counting of birds. A more plausible explanation is that the thick-soled species uses it as a method for burning off calories stored up from excessive winter feeding.

LBJ is a term used by birders to refer to the countless number of similar-looking "little brown jobs."

There was an Old Man with a beard,
Who said, "It is just as I feared! —
Two Owls and a Hen,
Four Larks and a Wren,
Have all built their nests in my beard!"

EDWARD LEAR, English writer and artist
Book of Nonsense (1846)

Drawings on both pages by Edward Lear (self-portrait above)

BILL ME

Each word below can be combined with one other to spell the name of a bird. Put together the 12 bird names, then transfer them to the spaces on the next page to find out whose bill is whose.

AGER	FISHER	MOUSE	ROT
CATCHER	HATCH	NUT	SKIM
DART	HER	ON	STAR
EON	KING	PAR	TAN
ER	LING	PECKER	TIT
FLY	MER	PIG	WOOD

_____   _____

_____   _____

_____   _____

_____   _____

_____   _____

_____   _____

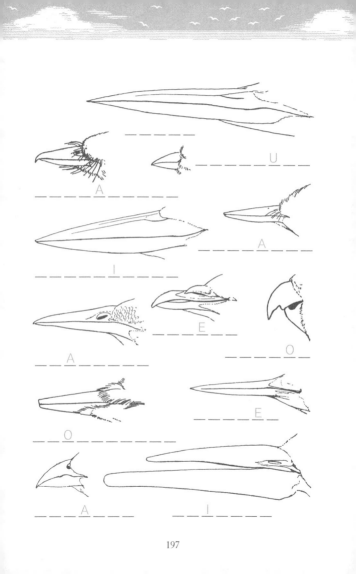

U

A

A

I

A

E

O

O

E

A

I

BILL ME

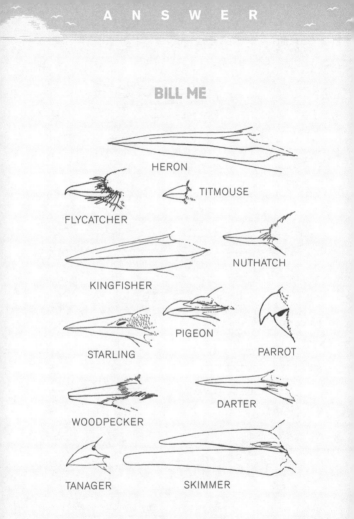

HERON

TITMOUSE

FLYCATCHER

KINGFISHER

NUTHATCH

STARLING

PIGEON

PARROT

WOODPECKER

DARTER

TANAGER

SKIMMER

ANTING is a behavior where birds rub ants or other insects over their feathers. Hundreds of species do it, perhaps using the ants' secretions as a parasite repellent, a preening aid, or even an intoxicant. It might also be a way of wiping acid off the ants before eating them.

Tanagers (right) use *active anting*, rubbing themselves with ants. Others, such as waxbills and crows, use *passive anting*, where they lay on an anthill and let the ants crawl over them.

The Birds

. . . is a title or name that has been used by
a varied group of artists over the years.

414 BCE Aristophanes' play featured a
chorus of birds that directly addresses the
audience, at one point promising not to
defecate on them if they
give the play first prize.

1927 Composer
Ottorino Respighi's
musical suite was
based on the work
of five 18th-century
composers who'd
put birdsong into
musical notation.

1952 Daphne du Maurier's novelette told of the English countryside being attacked by massive numbers of birds.

1953–54 A radio version of du Maurier's story was heard on two popular radio anthology series, the *Lux Radio Theater* in 1953 and *Escape* in 1954.

1963 Alfred Hitchcock's classic movie, based on du Maurier's story, opened the Cannes Film Festival. Ads for it proclaimed, "The Birds is coming!"

1964 A British rock band was formed, including future Rolling Stone Ron Wood. After a quick start they were soon eclipsed by the similarly named American band, The Byrds, and disbanded in 1967.

There is a legend about a bird which sings just once in its life, more sweetly than any other creature on the face of the earth. From the moment it leaves the nest it searches for a thorn tree, and does not rest until it has found one. Then, singing among the savage branches, it impales itself upon the longest, sharpest spine. And, dying, it rises above its own agony to out-carol the lark and the nightingale. One superlative song, existence the price. But the whole world stills to listen, and God in His heaven smiles. For the best is only bought at the price of great pain.... Or so says the legend.

COLLEEN McCULLOUGH
The Thorn Birds (1977)

CHIMNEY SWIFTS
actually benefited at first
from European settlement in the
New World. The construction
of chimneys gave them many
more nesting sites.

QUIP TIME

These three quips are all written using the same letter substitution code. One letter stands for another: For example, W = L. Quip #1 is by Milton Berle. Quips #2 and #3 are by Steven Wright.

1. OIM HJF WTGZ JU

   HRZJXWS JU MFZ,

   TN MFZ TU J RMBUZ

   JFY ORZ MORZB J

   UXJBBMI.

2. T HJF WZGTOJOZ

   DTBYU. FM MFZ HJBZU.

3. TCJKTFZ TN DTBYU

   IZBZ OTHAWZY DS

   NZJORZBU.

QUIP TIME

1. Two can live as cheaply as one, if one is a horse and the other a sparrow.
2. I can levitate birds. No one cares.
3. Imagine if birds were tickled by feathers.

THE
KIWI,
a fuzzy
pear-shaped
bird that serves
as New Zealand's
unofficial symbol, is
not only flightless, it's
also the only bird in
the world that has
no wings.

Bird Jokes

Jokes to share with a kid you know...
or an adult who hasn't grown up yet.

10

Q: Why don't seagulls live on bays?
A: Because then they'd be bagels.

9

Q: Why do storks stand on one leg?
A: If they lifted both legs, they'd fall down.

8

Q: What was the name of the
mathematician's lost parrot?
A: Polygon.

7

Q: What did the roadrunner say when it
walked into a bar?
A: Ouch!

6

Q: What do chickens throw but baseball players hit?

A: Fowl (foul) balls.

5

Q: Why was the bird's beak green with the number "1" written all over it?

A: It was a one-dollar bill.

4

Q: What vegetable do baby birds like best?

A: Chick peas.

3

Q: How can you avoid whooping cranes?

A: By not picking fights with them.

2

Q: What do you call a sticky black bird?

A: Velcrow.

1

Q: Why did the baby canary cost less?

A: Because it was a little cheeper.

HANSEL AND GRETEL
without birds?
No story.

1. The forest birds eat the duo's bread crumb trail, preventing them from finding their way back home.

2. A white bird appears and lures them to the witch's gingerbread house.

3. After baking the crone, the only way for the wayward naifs to cross a big expanse of water that separates them from their home is on the back of a white duck.

A bird does not
sing because it
has an answer,
it sings because
it has a song.

- - - - - - - - - - - - - -

MAYA ANGELOU
(born 1928)

BIRDOKU 2

These nine letters fill
the grid nine times each:

OWL DESIGN

Each letter must appear once in each row,
in each column, and in each 3×3 square.

The three words highlighted in green, reading
down, will spell out the answer to this riddle:

What does a flying goose
use for slowing down?

_____   _____   ____

	G	L	N		D	I		E
E								N
	W	N	E		I		D	
		G		D	S		W	
D	E						L	S
	O		W	E		G		
	N		G		E	D	O	
L								G
G		O	L		N	S	E	

BIRDOKU 2

O	G	L	N	W	D	I	S	E
E	I	D	S	L	O	W	G	N
S	W	N	E	G	I	L	D	O
N	L	G	O	D	S	E	W	I
D	E	W	I	N	G	O	L	S
I	O	S	W	E	L	G	N	D
W	N	I	G	S	E	D	O	L
L	S	E	D	O	W	N	I	G
G	D	O	L	I	N	S	E	W

SLOW WING DOWN

214

EGGS that aren't white receive their coloring and patterns several hours prior to being laid. The mother produces the pigments by breaking down hemoglobin from burst red blood cells in her body.

I paint . . .
as a bird sings.

CLAUDE MONET
(1840–1926)

PABLO PICASSO, who grew up surrounded by the pigeons his father raised, chose them as the subject of some of his earliest drawings and continued to draw them throughout his life.

In 1949, a pigeon in his sketchbook was picked to be the symbol for the Paris World Peace Conference.

When Picasso's daughter was born in 1949, he had the perfect name for her — Paloma, which means "pigeon" in Spanish.

Audubon, the Hunter

During his artistic quest, John James Audubon hunted and killed countless numbers of birds — to study them, compare individuals, perform autopsies, and, perhaps most often, to pose them for his paintings, usually using mounting wires to position them more naturally.

On one occasion his take was 115 chimney swallows at rest in a hollow Kentucky sycamore in order to perform a population count. Another time, during a two-week trek in the swamps of New

Jersey, he collected 300 whip-poor-wills, nighthawks, fishhawks, and other birds, the skins of which were sold to museums to help finance his expeditions and to support his family.

One inescapable reality of life in the wilderness was a need to eat, and Audubon often saw his daily catches serving double duty as nighttime meals. His field notes on ducks regularly included reviews of their palatability. Other birds were consumed as well. A supper of 16 starlings proved to be "good & delicate" while grebes were judged "extremely fishy, rancid and fat." He likewise deemed one goose "extremely fishy," while a hermit thrush made for "fat and delicate eating."

ODD BIRDS

Twenty birds with somewhat unusual names have been hidden in the grid. Look for them reading left, right, up, down, and diagonally in all directions.

ANTPITTA	KAKAPO
BARBET	KERERU
BOOBOOK	LORY
BULBUL	MAMO
CROMBEC	PHALAROPE
FRANCOLIN	PIOPIO
GERYGONE	PITOHUI
HOATZIN	PO'OULI
HOOPOE	TINAMOU
JACANA	VANGA

```
P  O  M  I  R  Z  A  K  A  O  P  H
A  I  V  A  A  N  G  E  B  U  M  B
M  O  O  F  T  E  N  R  T  I  U  O
O  A  P  P  T  V  A  E  E  L  H  Z
I  H  M  O  I  B  V  R  B  U  O  I
T  H  O  O  P  O  E  U  R  I  A  N
I  O  P  E  T  O  L  Z  A  T  T  H
N  R  J  J  N  B  M  O  B  H  Z  N
A  L  A  O  A  O  O  U  P  H  I  I
M  H  C  N  P  O  O  U  L  I  N  L
O  P  A  K  A  K  J  I  E  Z  T  O
U  H  N  V  O  C  E  B  M  O  R  C
J  Y  A  Y  Y  S  G  Y  N  A  K  N
O  G  E  R  Y  G  O  N  E  V  Z  A
U  A  O  J  P  I  T  O  H  U  I  R
M  L  E  P  O  R  A  L  A  H  P  F
```

ODD BIRDS

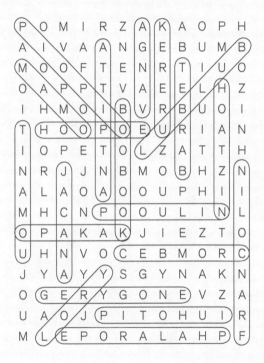

MIGRATING BIRDS navigate using the sun, stars, landmarks, the earth's magnetic field, and even their sense of smell. Some species are born with a "map" programmed into their brains. Others need to be shown the way the first time but can then replicate the route from memory.

The Novice Birder

Least Bitter

Buffalo Head

Showy Egret

Coldfinch

Goodwit

Grossbeak

Rough Grouse

Great Blue Herring

Castrol

Browned Pelican

Black Scooter

Common Sniper

European Sterling

Dusty Thrush

Downed Woodpecker

Minor bird

The Seasoned Birder

Least Bittern

Bufflehead

Snowy Egret

Goldfinch

Godwit

Grosbeak

Ruffed Grouse

Great Blue Heron

Kestrel

Brown Pelican

Black Scoter

Common Snipe

European Starling

Dusky Thrush

Downy Woodpecker

Myna bird

Oh, I love pigeons more than anything else in this world . . . besides oatmeal.

- - - - -

BERT

Sesame Street (1969)

Passenger Pigeons

Although once flying in flocks estimated at 1 to 2 *billion* birds, likely the world's most abundant bird species, the last American passenger pigeon died in the Cincinnati Zoo on September 1, 1914. Her name was Martha, named for Martha Washington.

A century prior to that, John J. Audubon entered this description of a Kentucky swarm in his journal: "The air was literally filled with Pigeons; the light of noonday was obscured as by an eclipse . . . and the continued buzz of wings had a tendency to lull my senses to repose."

Alas, mass hunting for the market, loss of habitat, and the birds' inability to adequately reproduce in small groups led to the passenger pigeon's demise.

REAL NAMES

Eight real bird names have been split in two.
Put them back together using the punny clues.

AMERICAN	COOT	JAY	SAGE
BANK	CREEPER	KING	SCRUB
BROWN	GREAT	KNOT	SWALLOW
CHICKEN	HAWK	RAIL	THRASHER

Tonight Show bath
attendant's order _____

Dried-up vine _____

Old U.S. citizen _____

Teller's gulp _____

Big tie-up _____

Brainy hitter _____

Ruler's staircase aid _____

Timid warmonger _____

FAKE NAMES

Eight of these 15 bird names are fakes.
Can you pick out all the imposters?

REAL		FAKE
_____	Black-whiskered vireo	_____
_____	Five-striped sparrow	_____
_____	Gull-winged delorean	_____
_____	Sharp-shinned hawk	_____
_____	Olive-sided flycatcher	_____
_____	Flat-footed booby	_____
_____	Nose-ringed parakeet	_____
_____	Long-haired catbird	_____
_____	Yellow-rumped warbler	_____
_____	Pot-bellied plover	_____
_____	Double-dipped scaup	_____
_____	Yellow-nosed albatross	_____
_____	Brown-throated wren	_____
_____	Pipe-billed grebe	_____
_____	Swallowed-tail kite	_____

REAL NAMES

Scrub jay
Brown creeper
American coot
Bank swallow
Great knot
Sage thrasher
King rail
Chicken hawk

FAKE NAMES

The fakes are:
Gull-winged delorean
Flat-footed booby
Nose-ringed parakeet
Long-haired catbird
Pot-bellied plover
Double-dipped scaup
Pipe-billed grebe
Swallowed-tail kite

One morn the wind blowed cold and strong,
And the Leaves went whirling away;
The birds prepared for their journey long,
That raw and gusty day.

HENRY DAVID THOREAU
(1817–62)

It's Official

(a) Since the purple martin, a bird known for its appetite for flying insects, is deemed by most as an attractive asset for its appearance, song, cleanliness, and diet — America's Most Wanted Bird, and since the City of Lake Village in Chicot County of southeastern Arkansas is located along the North-South Flyway, the major migration route for millions of birds, the City of Lake Village in Chicot County, shall be designated by the General Assembly to be known as the "Southeast Purple Martin Capital of the State of Arkansas."

(b) The City of Fort Smith is hereby designated as the "Northwest Purple Martin Capital of Arkansas."

Get a Grip

Grip, a pet raven belonging to Charles Dickens, was an inspirational force behind two notable works. A talking raven of the same name appeared in Dickens' 1841 novel, *Barnaby Rudge.* In a review of the book, Edgar Allan Poe felt the bird should have loomed even larger. Four years later, he put that thought into action when he wrote "The Raven."

A preserved and mounted Grip currently resides in the Rare Book Department of the Free Library of Philadephia. In 1999, it was designated a "literary landmark" by the Friends of Library USA.

"What was that? Him tapping at the door?"

CHARLES DICKENS
the widow speaking in *Barnaby Rudge* (1841)

"'Tis some visitor," I muttered, "tapping at my chamber door . . ."

EDGAR ALLAN POE
"The Raven" (1845)

NO WAL-KING

Shahnameh, a Persian epic written in 1000 CE, tells of King Kai Kavus's unusual mode of transportation. To discover what it is, answer the clues, then transfer the letters to the same-numbered spaces in the grid.

1D	2B		3B	4D	5J	6F	7H	8K	9L	10E
11J	12C		13B	14F	15H	16E	17C		18L	19E
20D	21F	22G	23J		24K	25B		26C	27G	28H
29J	30K	31E	32A	33G	34B	35D		36A	37K	
38B	39H	40G		41B	42L	43C	44G	45A	46J	
47D	48H	49F	50E	51H	52L	53C		54L	55A	
56F	57J	58C	59G	60E		61E	62F		63H	64J

A. "High" time of day

‾‾ ‾‾ ‾‾ ‾‾
45   36   55   32

B. Part of a bird that might be left behind

‾‾ ‾‾ ‾‾ ‾‾ ‾‾ ‾‾ ‾‾
25   2   3   41   38   13   34

C. Time when many orioles vacation in Mexico

$\overline{}_{53}$ $\overline{}_{58}$ $\overline{}_{12}$ $\overline{}_{26}$ $\overline{}_{17}$ $\overline{}_{43}$

D. Really dislikes

$\overline{}_{1}$ $\overline{}_{47}$ $\overline{}_{4}$ $\overline{}_{20}$ $\overline{}_{35}$

E. "Sunshine State" that can precede scrub jay

$\overline{}_{50}$ $\overline{}_{16}$ $\overline{}_{19}$ $\overline{}_{31}$ $\overline{}_{61}$ $\overline{}_{10}$ $\overline{}_{60}$

F. Country's name that can precede goose

$\overline{}_{56}$ $\overline{}_{14}$ $\overline{}_{62}$ $\overline{}_{6}$ $\overline{}_{49}$ $\overline{}_{21}$

G. Already picked, as a mate

$\overline{}_{22}$ $\overline{}_{27}$ $\overline{}_{44}$ $\overline{}_{40}$ $\overline{}_{33}$ $\overline{}_{59}$

H. Room topper or bird's maximum altitude

$\overline{}_{7}$ $\overline{}_{28}$ $\overline{}_{63}$ $\overline{}_{51}$ $\overline{}_{39}$ $\overline{}_{48}$ $\overline{}_{15}$

J. Hand ax

$\overline{}_{57}$ $\overline{}_{11}$ $\overline{}_{64}$ $\overline{}_{29}$ $\overline{}_{23}$ $\overline{}_{46}$ $\overline{}_{5}$

K. Horseshoe's spot

$\overline{}_{8}$ $\overline{}_{24}$ $\overline{}_{30}$ $\overline{}_{37}$

L. Scarce hen items

$\overline{}_{18}$ $\overline{}_{9}$ $\overline{}_{52}$ $\overline{}_{54}$ $\overline{}_{42}$

NO WAL-KING

A. NOON
B. FEATHER
C. WINTER
D. HATES
E. FLORIDA
F. CANADA

G. CHOSEN
H. CEILING
J. HATCHET
K. HOOF
L. TEETH

HE ATTACHED
AN EAGLE TO
EACH OF THE
CORNERS OF
HIS THRONE
AND FLEW TO
CHINA IN IT

THE HOODED PITOHUI
of New Guinea possesses a
very rare avian defense —
poisonous feathers and skin.

The bright orange and black
bird doesn't produce the toxin
itself but is thought to acquire
it from the beetles it eats.

Although pronounced
"pit-o-hooey," a more apt
pronunciation of its name
might be "pit-oo-ey."

Flapping Extremes

FASTEST:
Hummingbird

- -

200 beats/second during
courtship displays and
power dives

SLOWEST:
Albatross

- -

Can glide for hours
without a single beat
of its wings

Wingspan Extremes

LARGEST:
Albatross

Up to 12 feet for
for the wandering
albatross

SMALLEST:
Hummingbird

As little as 2½ inches
for the bee
hummingbird

Orioles hang,

Owls hide;

Grebes float,

Duck inside.

A bird seems to be at the top of the scale, so vehement and intense his life . . . The beautiful vagabonds, endowed with every grace, masters of all climes, and knowing no bounds — how many human aspirations are realised in their free, holiday-lives.

JOHN BURROUGHS
American naturalist (1837–1921)

A LOT AND NOT

In this puzzle you'll find eight short bird names that appear quite often in crosswords and four well-known birds with longer names that rarely do.

ACROSS

1 "O Sole ___"
4 Some shirt sizes (abbr.)
7 Spider's meal fetcher
10 Haul
11 Small songbird
12 *Little Women* woman
13 Bird Snoopy imitates
15 Regret
16 Word ending in -ly
18 Large boats
21 Prefix with -lithic
24 Deceive
26 Rudder's location
27 Brainteaser
28 Sea eagle
29 Camera stand
32 It causes inflation
34 Fastest bird on land
38 Put to work
39 Long. crosser
40 So-so grade
41 ___ Kan pet foods
42 W.W. II arena
43 Hither's partner

DOWN

1 Teen tube favorite
2 Poker game chit
3 It gives a hoot
4 Formal shirt fastener
5 Nuclear missile, briefly
6 Brews tea
7 Common American bird
8 Outback runner
9 "So long"
14 Worried king's employee
17 Like a very violent movie
18 European peak
19 Carnival city
20 Bird of prey that hovers
22 Variation of 28-Across
23 "The loneliest number"
25 Hanging nest maker
30 H.S. junior's exam
31 Palindromic fellow
32 Cliff-dwelling bird
33 "This ___ joke, right?"
35 Frigid
36 Corporate bigwig
37 Cock's mate

BONUS SCRAMBLER

Unscramble the letters in the light green squares to find a common bird that's uncommon in crosswords.

— — — — — — — — —

A LOT AND NOT

M	I	O		S	M	S		W	E	B
T	O	W		T	I	T		A	M	Y
V	U	L	T	U	R	E		R	U	E
			A	D	V	E	R	B		
A	R	K	S			P	A	L	E	O
L	I	E	T	O		S	T	E	R	N
P	O	S	E	R		E	R	N	E	
		T	R	I	P	O	D			
A	I	R		O	S	T	R	I	C	H
U	S	E		L	A	T		C	E	E
K	A	L		E	T	O		Y	O	N

Bonus Scrambler: MEADOWLARK

EMU

. . . is the most frequently appearing bird in *The New York Times* crossword. Overall, it's been the 208th most common answer word found in their daily and Sunday puzzles during the last 15 years, appearing about two times every three months. Rounding out the top 15 birds, in descending order of frequency, are:

ERN, HEN, ERNE, NENE,
RHEA, IBIS, TEAL, ORIOLE,
EAGLE, WREN, EGRET,
EIDER, LOON, and TERN.

DOES THE EARLY BIRD GET THE WORM?

Worms tend to be most active near the surface during early morning hours — so, yes.

Worms also often come to the surface during rainstorms and to mate, so the early wet voyeur bird really has it made.

To even mention all the things the bird must constantly keep in mind in order to fly securely through the air would take a considerable part of the evening . . . The bird has learned this art of equilibrium, and learned it so thoroughly that its skill is not apparent to our sight. We only learn to appreciate it when we try to imitate it.

WILBUR WRIGHT
Speech to the Western Society of Engineers (1901)

If I had to choose, I would rather have birds than airplanes.

CHARLES LINDBERGH
Reader's Digest, "Is Civilization Progress?"
(July 1964)

BOB'S BIRD BARN

Five friends live on Bay Boulevard. The first lives one bus stop from Bob's Bird Barn. The others are two, three, four, and five stops away from Bob's.

One day, they each decide to take the Bay Boulevard bus to Bob's to buy a bluebird costing $5 and a box of Bob's Birdseed also costing $5.

If it costs 20¢ to travel between each bus stop, and the five women together have a total of $55, will there be enough money for all of their round trip fares and Bird Barn purchases? If not, how much extra will they have, or need?

BOB'S BIRD BARN

The total money needed is $56, so they'd be short by $1. Here's how it totals up:

Purchases at Bob's = $50
  5 bluebirds @ $5 each = $25
  5 boxes of birdseed @ $5 each = $25

Round trips = $6
  1st woman = 40¢ (20¢ each way)
  2nd woman = 80¢
  3rd woman = $1.20
  4th woman = $1.60
  5th woman = $2.00

ALFRED HITCHCOCK'S
The Birds was filled with the
sounds of birds — all of which
were artificially created using
an electronic instrument called
a trautonium. It was the only
"music" used in the film.

God loved the birds
and invented trees.
Man loved the birds
and invented cages.

JACQUES DEVAL
French playwright (1895–1975)

A Robin Redbreast
in a Cage puts all
Heaven in a Rage.

WILLIAM BLAKE
English poet (1757–1827)

You know, at one time I used to break into pet shops and liberate the canaries, but I decided that was an idea way before its time. Zoos are full, prisons are overflowing. Ah, my. How the world still dearly loves a cage.

RUTH GORDON
Harold and Maude (1971)

*There is nothing
in which the birds
differ more from
man than the way
in which they can
build and yet leave
a landscape as it
was before.*

ROBERT WILSON LYND
British writer (1879–1949)

BEAKS AND FEATHERS

are both made of keratin,
similar to our fingernails
and hair. A bird's feathers
are dead matter, while its
beak, with blood vessels
and nerves inside, is alive
and continually growing.

STUMPERS

The words below are spelled using the letters in BIRD BRAINTEASERS. There's only one way to fit them all in the grid.

3 letters

ATE   INS
BEE   NET

4 letters

AREA   NEST   TIDE
BAIT   SEED
EAST   TERN

5 letters

BEATS
DENSE
RISEN
TREES

6 letters

BARBED
BARREN
BREAST
DARTER
EATERS

7 letters

DAISIES
SEASIDE
TERRAIN

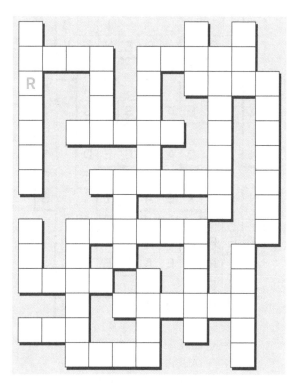

STUMPERS

A few anagrams of BIRD BRAINTEASERS:

RABBIT DREARINESS

IBIS REDBREAST RAN

ARAB BIRDS IN TREES

LIGHT RECEPTORS that help birds decide when to migrate aren't in their eyes — they're in the middle of their brains, analyzing the slight yet differing amounts of light that make it through the surrounding layers.

WHAT OTHER ANIMAL can be drawn with a single stroke of the pen and still be instantly recognized?

*If one cannot
catch a bird of
paradise, better
take a wet hen.*

NIKITA KHRUSHCHEV
(1894–1971)

"I think that's the flock that grazes
over by the Volkswagen plant."

Formations

The reasons birds fly in formation are thought to be twofold:

1. To conserve energy (great white pelicans, for example, use up to 14% less energy when trailing others)
2. To maintain good communication, visually and perhaps even vocally

The most common are V formations, varying from broad wedges to those that pierce the sky like a dagger. Other birds prefer to fly in J formations or in a gently arcing bow shape.

HEAD SCRATCHERS 3

1. A researcher was studying rhinos and the oxpecker birds that eat ticks off them. One day, in a small clearing, she counted 40 heads and 100 legs between the two species. How many rhinos and how many birds were there?

2. Each of these birds is missing at least one of each vowel, A, E, I, O, and U:

MNTN BLBRD _____

BLCK-BLLD CCK _____

SHRP-TLD GRS _____

DBN'S RL _____

3. Adding one letter at a time, so that a new word is spelled on each line, can you get from "I" to STARLING? The new letter can be inserted anywhere, but the letter order from the previous word can't be changed.

I

___ ___

___ ___ ___

___ ___ ___ ___

___ ___ ___ ___ ___

___ ___ ___ ___ ___ ___

___ ___ ___ ___ ___ ___ ___

S T A R L I N G

HEAD SCRATCHERS 3

1. There were 10 rhinos and 30 birds. The 10 rhinos would account for 40 legs; the 30 birds would account for 60 legs.
2. MOUNTAIN BLUEBIRD
   BLACK-BILLED CUCKOO
   SHARP-TAILED GROUSE
   AUDUBON'S ORIOLE
3. I - IN - SIN - SING - STING
   STRING - STARING - STARLING

The Humming-Bird
is the Miracle of all
our wing'd Animals;
He is feather'd as a Bird,
and gets his Living as
the Bees, by sucking
the Honey from
each Flower.

JOHN LAWSON
A New Voyage to Carolina (1709)

THE KOOKABURRA

is unique to Australia, and yet its exotic and eerie call was an integral part of the African jungle noises heard in the old Tarzan movies.

FREE TEST REVEALS
YOUR ART TALENT

What's a thousand dollars? Mere chicken feed. A poultry matter.

GROUCHO MARX
The Cocoanuts (1929)

Have you got any milk-fed chickens?

Yes, sir.

Well, squeeze the milk out of one and bring me a glass.

GROUCHO MARX
A Night at the Opera (1935)

BBs

Like "bird brain," each of these answers has the initials BB. Use the clues to fill in each answer, then read down the circled letters to complete this sentence:

A crow's brain-to-body ratio is ...

1. Karate pro
2. Tossed wedding flowers
3. Pushpin site
4. Dish often served with franks
5. 12 oz. Bud container
6. Navel
7. Wild horse tamer
8. One born in the '50s
9. Child's construction cube
10. Recover quickly
11. Alley roller
12. Sack that potatoes come in
13. Oath-sharing men
14. London timekeeper
15. Female gymnast's apparatus
16. One always on the go

1. B _ _ _ _   B _ _ _

2. B _ _ _ _ _ ' _   B _ _ _ _ _ _

3. B _ _ _ _ _ _ _ _   B _ _ _ _

4. B _ _ _ _   B _ _ _ _

5. B _ _ _   B _ _ _ _ _

6. B _ _ _ _   B _ _ _ _ _

7. B _ _ _ _ _   B _ _ _ _ _

8. B _ _ _   B _ _ _ _ _

9. B _ _ _ _ _ _ _   B _ _ _ _

10. B _ _ _ _ _   B _ _ _

11. B _ _ _ _ _ _   B _ _ _

12. B _ _ _ _ _   B _ _

13. B _ _ _ _   B _ _ _ _ _ _

14. B _ _   B _ _

15. B _ _ _ _ _ _   B _ _ _

16. B _ _ _   B _ _

BBs

1. BLACK BELT
2. BRIDE'S BOUQUET
3. BULLETIN BOARD
4. BAKED BEANS
5. BEER BOTTLE
6. BELLY BUTTON
7. BRONCO BUSTER
8. BABY BOOMER
9. BUILDING BLOCK
10. BOUNCE BACK
11. BOWLING BALL
12. BURLAP BAG
13. BLOOD BROTHERS
14. BIG BEN
15. BALANCE BEAM
16. BUSY BEE

A crow's brain-to-body ratio is ...

EQUAL TO A DOLPHIN'S

(And it's only slightly less
than a human's.)

LEWIS CARROLL included himself in *Alice in Wonderland* — in the form of a dodo bird. Dodo was a childhood nickname that resulted from Carroll's stuttering pronunciation of his real last name, Dodgson.

Hi, kids! My name is Harry Recon, and this is my twin sister, Aerial. She's going to tell you about the History of the CIA.

Hey gang. I'm Aerial, the ace photography pigeon. Did you know pigeons were once used to take secret pictures?

HARRY AND AERIAL RECON
from the kid's page on the CIA's Web site
(2001, 2007)

Meadowfinch

For the state of Washington, settling
on a state bird took a bit of doing.

1928: The state's school children voted and
overwhelmingly chose the meadowlark.

1931: Since the meadowlark was already
the state bird of seven other states, the
Washington Federation of Women's Clubs
held another vote. This time the willow
goldfinch was the clear winner.

1931–51: Washington had two state birds,
the meadowlark and goldfinch.

1951: The state's school children voted one
last time and chose the willow goldfinch,
which the Legislature unanimously
ratified as Washington's sole state bird.

WHAT'S IN A NAME?

Pigeons are denigrated by some as "flying rats" while doves are revered as the very symbols of peace — and yet they are the same bird.

The common city pigeon's original name was the rock dove.

*I know people think
I'm crazy, some black,
young millionaire in
this abandoned building
flying pigeons, but . . .
I've been doing this
longer than anything
I've ever participated in
besides breathing.*

MIKE TYSON

Former boxing champ on *Jimmy Kimmel Live!* (April 2003).
Tyson spends 18 hours some days tending his 1,100 birds.

GREEN EGGS, AGAIN

Start at the blue egg in the upper left and move *diagonally*, stopping at any green egg. From that green egg, move diagonally to another green egg. Continuing in this fashion, find a path to the blue egg in the upper right.

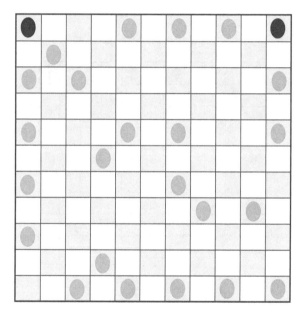

GREEN EGGS, AGAIN

Here's the shortest route:

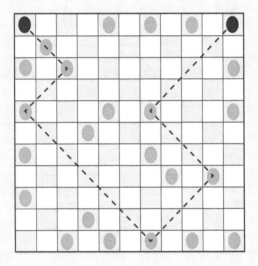

*It is not only
fine feathers that
make fine birds.*

AESOP (620–560 BCE)

Woodcut of Aesop from the *Nuremberg Chronicle* (1493)

Posted
Pine Knot
Preserve

Discovered

Turkey hunting in the Old Dominion

This 1906 cartoon shows Teddy Roosevelt sparing the lives of two domestic turkeys put out as a prank by neighbors near his Virginia hunting lodge, Pine Knot. The joke was inspired by the famous incident when Roosevelt had refused to shoot a bear cub tied to a tree.

Bully for Birds

Teddy Roosevelt spent countless hours of his youth studying, drawing, and learning the songs of birds. At the age of 15, while in Germany, he spent much of his time dissecting and cataloging the local birds. Four years later, back in the U.S., he and a friend published "The Summer Birds of the Adirondacks in Franklin County, N.Y.," a four-page catalog of their observations made over three summers.

Roosevelt's ornithological interests continued as president. In 1903, he created the first federal bird reserve at Florida's Pelican Island. By the time he left office 50 more had been added, as well as four game reserves and 150 national forests. All told, Roosevelt put more than 230 million acres of land under federal protection, an area larger than the 13 original colonies.

Revenge of the
Thanksgiving
Turkey

Along about midnight, Nemo thought he felt the house tremble . . .

Their home was slowly but surely ascending skyward but by what mysterious power Nemo's papa could not make out. Nemo suggested that it might be some monster giant but his papa called him a "rattlebrain" and ordered him to pacify his mama who was making elaborate plans to faint. But Nemo's suggestion was a fact and before he could warn his parents he lost his balance and fell.

Fortunately, a lake of nice springy cranberry sauce received him without harm.

WINSOR McCAY
Excerpt from *Little Nemo in Slumberland*
Sunday newspaper comic (Thanksgiving week, 1905)

BIRDOKU 3

These nine letters fill
the grid nine times each:

PARK CUT MD

Each letter must appear once in each row,
in each column, and in each 3×3 square.

The five words highlighted in green, reading
down, will spell out the answer to this riddle:

What do you call a business
mogul's bird in a 5-ton transport?

—   — — —   — — — —

— — — — —   — — — —

C		K					R	
P	D	M		R	T	K		U
				P			D	A
				U			K	D
U		P	M		C	A		R
D	C		K					
K	M		R					
A		C	T	M		R	P	K
	P					T		M

BIRDOKU 3

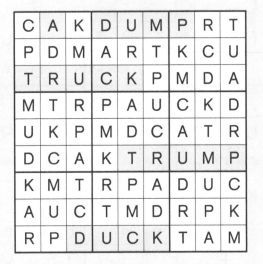

C	A	K	D	U	M	P	R	T
P	D	M	A	R	T	K	C	U
T	R	U	C	K	P	M	D	A
M	T	R	P	A	U	C	K	D
U	K	P	M	D	C	A	T	R
D	C	A	K	T	R	U	M	P
K	M	T	R	P	A	D	U	C
A	U	C	T	M	D	R	P	K
R	P	D	U	C	K	T	A	M

A DUMP TRUCK TRUMP DUCK

FLIGHTLESS BIRDS range in size from the nine-foot ostrich to a six-inch rail that lives on Inaccessible Island in the south Atlantic Ocean.

Tower Ravens

According to tradition, the Tower of London must always have six ravens in residence. Legend has it that King Charles II made the decree in the late 17th century when told the well-being of the tower and his entire kingdom depended on it.

Since 2006, the residents (the mandatory six plus three "extras") have been Baldrick, Bran, Branwen, Fleur, Guldulf, Gwyllum, Hugin, Munin, and Thor. A beefeater known as the Raven Master has the sole duty of tending to the birds, including feeding each a daily helping of raw meat and bird biscuits soaked in blood.

THE ORIGINAL PAINTINGS for *The Birds of America* were sold in 1863 by Audubon's widow to the New York Historical Society for $4,000. They spent the next 108 years stored in a basement.

THE COPPER PLATES met a mixed fate. Many were damaged in an 1845 fire, while others were given away. The majority, however, were sold as scrap metal to a Connecticut smelter in 1871. As workers were melting the plates down, the smeltery manager's 14-year-old son recognized what they were and managed to save about three dozen of them.

MINUS A TO Z

Unscramble the letters in each
equation to spell a bird's name.

MINERAL - A = _ _ _ _ _ _ _

RIBBON - B = _ _ _ _ _

CONCORD - C = _ _ _ _ _ _

HORNED - D = _ _ _ _ _

STROKE - E = _ _ _ _ _

FLOW - F = _ _ _

GNAWS - G = _ _ _ _

ANARCHY - H = _ _ _ _ _ _

DIAPER PINS - I = _ _ _ _ _ _ _ _ _

JOB DRIVEL - J = _ _ _ _ _ _ _ _

ROCK HITS - K = _ _ _ _ _ _ _

MANLY - L = _ _ _ _

TAPE MAKER - M = _ _ _ _ _ _ _ _ _

SURGEON - N = _ _ _ _ _ _ _

OWNER - O = _ _ _ _

GULPS ALE - P = _ _ _ _ _ _ _ _

MOST QUIET - Q = _ _ _ _ _ _ _ _ _

REGALE - R = _ _ _ _ _ _

GREETS - S = _ _ _ _ _ _

TAVERN - T = _ _ _ _ _

ICE CHUNK - U = _ _ _ _ _ _ _

CAVERN - V = _ _ _ _ _

VOWED - W = _ _ _ _

SEXY PRO - X = _ _ _ _ _ _ _

COWRY - Y = _ _ _ _

LIZARD CAN - Z = _ _ _ _ _ _ _ _ _

MINUS A TO Z

A	MERLIN	N	GROUSE
B	ROBIN	O	WREN
C	CONDOR	P	SEAGULL
D	HERON	Q	TITMOUSE
E	STORK	R	EAGLE
F	OWL	S	EGRET
G	SWAN	T	RAVEN
H	CANARY	U	CHICKEN
I	SANDPIPER	V	CRANE
J	LOVEBIRD	W	DOVE
K	OSTRICH	X	OSPREY
L	MYNA	Y	CROW
M	PARAKEET	Z	CARDINAL

*The perils of duck
hunting are great —
especially for the duck.*

WALTER CRONKITE
(born 1916)

Duck blind in Adak, Alaska

Bird Migration

...**ISN'T** simply about escaping the cold. Come fall, while other species are heading down the slopes of the Rockies and Sierras, the blue grouse is heading up. The lure? Conifer needles, which it feasts on throughout the winter.

... **DOESN'T** always involve flying. The great auk, now extinct, would swim from its breeding sites around Newfoundland to as far south as Florida. Emperor penguins will walk 125 miles, and emus as much as 300 miles, to breed.

EMILY DICKINSON
(1830–86)

A Bird came down the Walk:
He did not know I saw;
He bit an angle-worm in halves
And ate the fellow, raw.

I hope you
love birds too.
It is economical.
It saves going
to heaven.

Hope is the thing with feathers
That perches in the soul,
And sings the tune without
*   the words,*
And never stops at all.

AFTER BIRDS

Answers to asterisked (*) clues
are words that can follow "bird."

ACROSS

1 Phone*
5 DJ's playlist*
10 Operatic solo
11 Employer of barefoot
   stompers, perhaps
12 Intense anger
13 Loves
14 Along the way
16 Retired G.I.
17 Trojans sch.
18 Chest muscles, briefly
19 Seaside changing
   room*
22 Bonny girl
23 Hi-speed www link
24 One ___ million
25 Moulin Rouge
   exclamation
29 Putting cargo aboard
31 Spirit
32 Battery terminals
33 With 6-Down, Lennon's
   widow
34 Enclosures*
35 Farmer's purchase*

DOWN

1 Bistro
2 What a solo homer
   scores
3 Manhattan to Montauk
   line (abbr.)
4 Magazine designs
5 Slaw, in a diner, e.g.
6 See 33-Across
7 Jitteriness
8 First Olympics site
9 Wagering methods
   (abbr.)
11 Alpo-fed alarms*
15 Show to a seat,
   informally
18 Laundry line wheels
19 Chimp's treat
20 Sick ___ (really ailing)
21 ___Kosh B'Gosh
22 Light purple flower
25 Small bills
26 Soothing additive
27 Popular duck hangout
28 Give ___ to (approve)
30 Suffix with ox-

BONUS SCRAMBLER

Unscramble the letters in the light green squares to find a healthy snack whose two words can both follow "bird."

_ _ _ _ _   _ _ _ _

AFTER BIRDS

Both words in 19-Across and 11-Down
can follow "bird."

C	A	L	L			S	O	N	G	S
A	R	I	A		W	I	N	E	R	Y
F	U	R	Y		A	D	O	R	E	S
E	N	R	O	U	T	E		V	E	T
			U	S	C		P	E	C	S
	B	A	T	H	H	O	U	S	E	
L	A	S	S		D	S	L			
I	N	A		O	O	H	L	A	L	A
L	A	D	I	N	G		E	L	A	N
A	N	O	D	E	S		Y	O	K	O
C	A	G	E	S			S	E	E	D

Bonus Scrambler: BRAIN FOOD
(birdbrain, bird food)

A PENGUIN'S FEATHERS are more densely packed than any other bird, with about 70 tiny, flat feathers per square inch.

Jonathan Livingston Seagull...

Takes off: The book is published in 1970 and sells one million copies in two years.

Hits some turbulence: Some critics pan it as sentimental anthropomorphism.

Plummets: Moviegoers flock elsewhere when the big-screen version of the book is released in 1973. It brings in a paltry $1.6 million at the box office, and Richard Bach, the book's author, sues the filmmakers for veering from the book's text.

Rises back up: The movie receives Oscar nominations for cinematography and film editing, and Neil Diamond wins a Grammy for the film's music.

Soars: The book eventually sells 40 million copies, putting it in the top 50 of all-time best-selling books.

I want to fly where no seagull has flown before.

- - - - - - - -

The only true law is that which sets us free.

- - - - - - - -

There's got to be more to life than fighting for fish heads!

- -

JONATHAN, voiced by JAMES FRANCISCUS
from the movie version of *Jonathan Livingston Seagull* (1973)

"DISCO DUCK," a novelty song by Memphis deejay Rick Dees, hit #1 for a week in 1976. His station manager wasn't much of a fan, though. Dees was prohibited from playing the song on his show and was fired on the spot one day for merely mentioning it on the air.

To a man,
ornithologists
are tall, slender, and
bearded so that they
can stand motionless
for hours, imitating
kindly trees, as they
watch for birds.

GORE VIDAL
Armageddon? (1987)

A Final Thought

Manmade changes to the landscape are altering bird habitats across the planet in sudden and widespread ways. Global warming and the introduction of non-native species due to human activity only add to the problem. And the list of threats to birds goes on.

According to a 2006 study by Stuart Pimm of Duke University and his colleagues, 1,200 out of the approximately 10,000 known bird species aren't expected to make it to the end of the 21st century. An equal number might likely follow soon after.

Is it too late to reverse the trend?

No.

Bird conservation organizations

National Audubon Society
www.audubon.org

American Birding Association
www.americanbirding.org

American Bird Conservancy
www.abcbirds.org

Cornell Lab of Ornithology
www.birds.cornell.edu

North American Bird
Conservation Initiative
www.nabci-us.org

Bird Conservation Alliance
www.birdconservation
alliance.org

Wildlife conservation organizations

National Wildlife Federation
www.nwf.org

The Nature Conservancy
www.nature.org

World Wildlife Fund
wwf.panda.org

Sierra Club
www.sierraclub.org

U.S. government

EPA bird conservation page
http://water.epa.gov/type/wet-
lands/birds-index.cfm

Federal duck stamp program
www.fws.gov/duckstamps

Bird conservation books

Silence of the Songbirds
by Bridget Stutchbury

*Birder's Conservation
Handbook* by Jeffrey V. Wells

Two of my favorite bird books

And No Birds Sing
by Mark Jaffe

Living on the Wind
by Scott Weidensaul

Birdgo!

Next time you're out bird watching, here's a little game you can play. Photocopy the next page (or make multiple copies for your other birder pals) and see if you can cross off a straight line of five items, as in bingo. The line can run across, down, or diagonally.

When you've succeeded, yell out "Birdgo!" — but not too loudly or you'll scare away all the birds (and probably even a few people).

BIRDGO!

BROWN BIRD	ROBIN'S SONG	BIRD THAT STARTS WITH "G"	BIRDER WITH FANNY PACK	BIRD ON GRASS
2 BIRDS SINGING THE SAME SONG	BIRD FLYING ALONE	BIRD WITH BLUE FEATHERS	FINCH	BIRD THAT STARTS WITH "T"
BIRD OF PREY	BIRD WITH YELLOW FEATHERS	**FREE SPACE**	BIRD THAT STARTS WITH "S"	PAIR OF BIRDS FLYING
BIRD TAKING DUST BATH	BLACK BIRD	PIECE OF TRASH YOU PICK UP	BIRD WITH RED FEATHERS	WARBLER
BIRD THAT STARTS WITH "C"	BIRD'S NEST	HOPPING BIRD	BIRD ON A BRANCH	BIRD WITH WHITE FEATHERS

BIRD BRAINTEASERS by Patrick Merrell

You cannot prevent the birds of sorrow from flying over your head, but you can prevent them from building nests in your hair.

CHINESE PROVERB

PATRICK MERRELL is the author of 25 books, the illustrator of 150, a graphic designer, and a puzzlemaker for the *New York Times,* the *Los Angeles Times,* the *Wall Street Journal, Scientific American, People, Sports Illustrated, Mad,* National Wildlife Federation publications, the American Crossword Puzzle Tournament, and the World Puzzle Championship. His previous book from Storey is *Coffee Time.*

Merrell lives with his wife and daughter in Mount Vernon, New York, a suburb bordering New York City with the usual assortment of robins, cardinals, finches, mockingbirds, a few pileated woodpeckers, and one wild turkey.

Page:	Source:
18	*On The Genesis of Species* (1871), St. George Mivart
19	Photo by Paul Selden, director of the Paleontological Institute, Univ. of Kansas
32–33	Library of Congress (LOC), photo by Edward S. Curtis (1905)
48	LOC (1871)
57	"Illustrated London News, Vol 56" (1870), illustration by George C. Leighton
58	LBJ Library
71, 87	U.S. Fish & Wildlife Service (US F&W), illustrations by Bob Hines
72	US F&W, photo by Lee Karney
79	Permission of Stephen B. O'Brien, Jr., Fine Arts of Boston, broker of the sale www.americansportingart.com
89	Photo by A. Kniesel, Germany, GNU*
97	National Science Foundation (NSF), photo by Emily Stone
106–07	Oxford University Museum of Natural History, photo by Ballista, GNU*
113	Photo by permission of Rob & Jules
123	Photo by permission of Ren West
127	National Archives
129	"Sing a Song of Sixpence," Walter Crane (1909)
131	Photo by Laitche, Osaka, Japan
136	LOC, photo by Herbert E. French (1921)
137	LOC
162–63	Photos courtesy of NASA
171	US F&W, photo by Jim Clark
192	Fermi National Accelerator Laboratory
193	White House Press Office, photo by Yoichi R. Okamoto (01/09/69)

197–98   *Handbook of Birds of Eastern North America,*
         Frank M. Chapman (1895)
199   US F&W, illustration by Bob Hines
203, 242 *Nests and Eggs of North American Birds,*
         (1889) illustrations by Theodore Jasper
         and W. Otto Emerson
210   *Grimms' Tales,* Margaret Hunt (1914),
         illustration by John B. Gruelle
227   *Orthogenetic Evolution in the Pigeons* (1920),
         illustration by Hayashi and Toda
233   US F&W, photo by Bill French
250–51   U.S. Air Force
265   Photo courtesy of the U.S. Dept. of State
273   Photo by permission of David Iliff, GNU*
288   *The Washington Post* (Nov. 3, 1903),
         cartoon by Clifford K. Berryman
297   Photo by Viki Male
303   US F&W, photo by Palmer C. Sekora
304   *Game Birds of California* (1918),
         illustration by Louis Agassiz Fuertes
306   Daguerreogue by William C. North (1846)
311   NSF, photo by Mike Usher

Birds of America, T. Gilbert Pearson, The University
Society (1917): pages 28–29, 215; illustrations by Louis
Agassiz Fuertes: 11, 42, 47, 98; photo by H. T. Middleton:
120–121; photo by H. L. Dillaway: 159

OTHER STOREY BOOKS YOU WILL ENJOY

The Backyard Bird-Lover's Guide by Jan Mahnken
This gorgeously illustrated volume is brimming with information
about attracting, enjoying, and understanding 135 of North America's
most common species. You'll learn how to feed them, house them,
provide nesting materials, and keep them coming back year after year.
320 pages. Paper. ISBN 978-0-88266-927-4.

The Bird Watching Answer Book by Laura Erickson
Hundreds of questions answered by the experts
at the Cornell Lab of Ornithology.
400 pages. Flexibind. ISBN 978-1-60342-452-3.

Into the Nest by Laura Erickson and Marie Read
Get an intimate look into the family lives of your favorite birds – with
beautiful, close-up photography of over 50 birds and their fledglings,
nest building, brooding, courtship, and much more.
208 pages. Paper. ISBN 978-1-61212-229-8.

Nature Anatomy by Julia Rothman
This whimsical visual guide is packed with artful illustrations
and rich insights into our natural world, ranging from geology
and astronomy to zoology, weather, botany, and more!
224 pages. Paper with flaps. ISBN 978-1-61212-231-1.

What's That Bird?
by Joseph Choiniere and Claire Mowbry Golding
With this guide, you'll learn how birds eat, communicate, and even
breathe, as well as the best ways to observe birds, techniques for
keeping a bird journal, and how to protect endangered birds. And
family-friendly projects, such as building a nesting box, enhance your
birding experience.
128 pages. Paper. ISBN 978-1-58017-554-8.

These and other books from Storey Publishing are available
wherever quality books are sold or by calling 1-800-441-5700.
Visit us at *www.storey.com* or sign up for our newsletter
at *www.storey.com/signup*.